Longman Test Practice Kits

Science

Key Stage 2

Andy Bailey • Tim Franks

Series editors
Geoff Black and Stuart Wall

Titles available
Key Stage 2
English
Mathematics
Science

Key Stage 3
English
Mathematics
Science

Addison Wesley Longman Ltd,
Edinburgh Gate, Harlow,
CM20 2JE, England
and Associated Companies throughout the World

©Addison Wesley Longman 1998

All rights reserved; no part of this publication may be reproduced, stored in a retrieval system, or transmitted in any form or by any means, electronic, mechanical, photocopying, recording or otherwise without either the prior written consent of the Publishers or a licence permitting restricted copying in the United Kingdom issued by the Copyright Licensing Agency Ltd, 90 Tottenham Court Road, London, W1P 9HE.

First published 1998

ISBN 0582 31593-x

British Library Cataloguing-in-Publication Data
A catalogue record for this book is available from the British Library.

Set by 30 in 13/19 pt Frutiger light

Produced by Longman Singapore Publishers Pte.
Printed in Great Britain by Henry Ling Limited, at the Dorset Press, Dorchester, Dorset.

Table of contents

The Key Stage 2 National Tests iv
How they work iv
Levels of achievement iv

Using this book vi
Science at Key Stage 2 vi
Part 1 Self-check revision vi
Part 2 Test practice papers vi

Part 1 Self-check revision 1
Revision progress chart 1
Topics 1–10 3
Answers to self-check questions 42

Part 2 Test practice papers 45
Taking the practice tests 45
Marking the questions 45
Instructions 45
Words of command used in test questions 46
Test A (Levels 3–5) 47
Test B (Levels 3–5) 59
Answers to Test A and mark scheme 68
Answers to Test B and mark scheme 71
Marking grid and level chart 74

The Key Stage 2 National Tests

How they work

During Years 3 to 6 your child is at Key Stage 2 of the National Curriculum. Your child will study Science, Mathematics and English and in Year 6 they are tested in each of these subjects.

- These are written tests. Your child will take them in May at their own school. The tests are then sent to a marker who will decide what mark your child should be given.
- There are two test papers for Science, Paper A and Paper B. Each test lasts for 35 minutes.
- Your child will receive the results of these tests before the end of term. You will also receive a teacher's assessment of your child's work in the classroom.
- Your child's results will be given to you as a level. Your child will be given a level for their test results and for the teacher's assessment of your child.
- You will be given information about your child's levels by the school. You will also be given information about the results achieved by the other children in the school and children around the country. You will then be able to check your child's progress against other children of their age.

Levels of achievement

Each subject is divided into levels at Key Stage 2. In Science there are five levels (1 to 5) You can see from the diagram below that your child is expected to reach Level 4. Children who find progress very difficult are said to be working towards Level 1 (WT).

☐ Exceptional performance	Above Level 5
	Level 5
	Level 4
▨ Exceeded target for age group	Level 3
	Level 2
▩ Achieved target for age group	Level 1
▩ Working towards target for age group	

Levels of achievement at Key Stage 2

The graph shows the percentage of children who reached the different levels at the end of Key Stage 2 in the 1996 tests for Science.

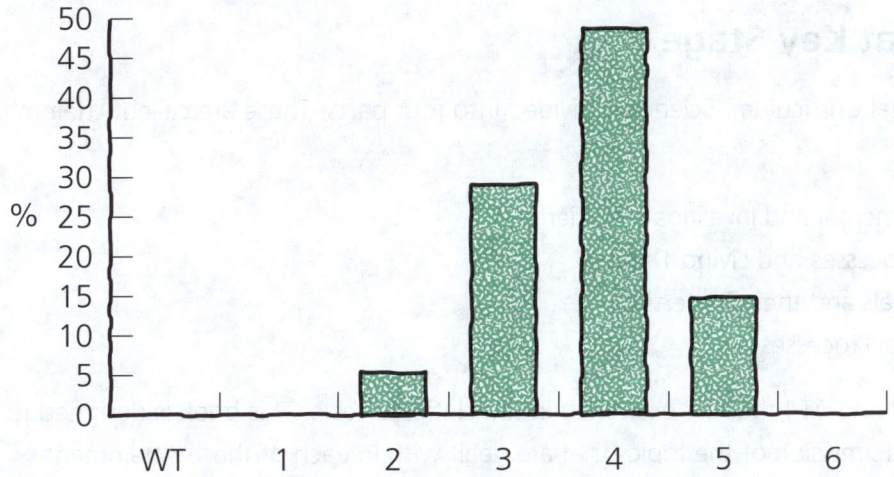

Percentage of 11 year-olds at each level in the National Science Test

Using this book

Science at Key Stage 2

In the National Curriculum, Science is divided into four parts. These are called Attainment Targets (ATs).

AT1 Experimental and Investigative Science
AT2 Life Processes and Living Things
AT3 Materials and their Properties
AT4 Physical Processes

It is AT2, AT3 and AT4 that are examined in the National Tests. This book is designed to aid your child's revision of the topics that are dealt with in each of these Attainment Targets, as listed in the 'Programme of Study' for Key Stage 2.

Part 1 Self-check revision

Part 1 (pages 1–44) of this book gives a brief outline of what your child should know under each of the topic headings tested at the end of Key Stage 2. Work through Part 1 together *before* you let your child try the practice tests in Part 2 of the book. To make this revision more interesting, your child will be given things to do. You can then tick off the topics that your child has revised in the chart on page 1.

Part 2 Test practice papers

Part 2 (pages 45–74) contains the following:

- **Words of command** Explanation of words used in questions on the Science Test Papers.
- **Questions** Two practice papers for Levels 3 to 5.
- **Answers and mark scheme** Answers to all of the questions, with a breakdown of the marks awarded.
- **Examiner tips** Helpful advice from the examiner to help your child improve their score.
- **Level chart** A guide to the marks needed to reach each level.

PART 1

Self-check revision

In this part of the book you will find a short, easy-to-use review of the key facts your child is expected to know for the National Test, as outlined in the Programme of Study. In this book we have organized the revision into 10 topics, which you should work through with your child.

To make your child's revision more interesting, they have to fill in blank spaces and answer questions. The answers to all the spaces and questions are at the end of this part, on pages 42–44.

After your child has revised a topic, and completed the spaces and questions in that topic, put a tick in the appropriate space in the following progress chart. This will help you to keep a record of your child's revision. Revise all of the topics in this part together *before* your child begins the test practice papers in Part 2.

Revision progress chart

		topic	tick when revised
LIFE PROCESSES	**1**	**Life processes, variation and classification**	
	1.1	Life processes	
	1.2	Variation and classification	
	2	**Humans as organisms**	
	2.1	Nutrition	
	2.2	Circulation	
	2.3	Movement	
	2.4	Growth and reproduction	
	2.5	Health	
	3	**Green plants as organisms**	
	3.1	Growth and nutrition	
	3.2	Reproduction	
	4	**Living things in their environment**	
	4.1	Adaptation	
	4.2	Feeding relationships	
	4.3	Micro-organisms	

	topic	tick when revised
MATERIALS		
5	**Grouping and classifying materials**	
6	**Changing materials**	
7	**Separating mixtures of materials**	
PHYSICAL PROCESSES		
8	**Electricity**	
9	**Forces and motion**	
9.1	Types of force	
9.2	Balanced and unbalanced forces	
9.3	The solar system	
10	**Light and sound**	
10.1	Everyday effects of light	
10.2	Seeing	
10.3	Vibration and sound	

Life processes, variation and classification

1.1 Life processes

These are all living things.

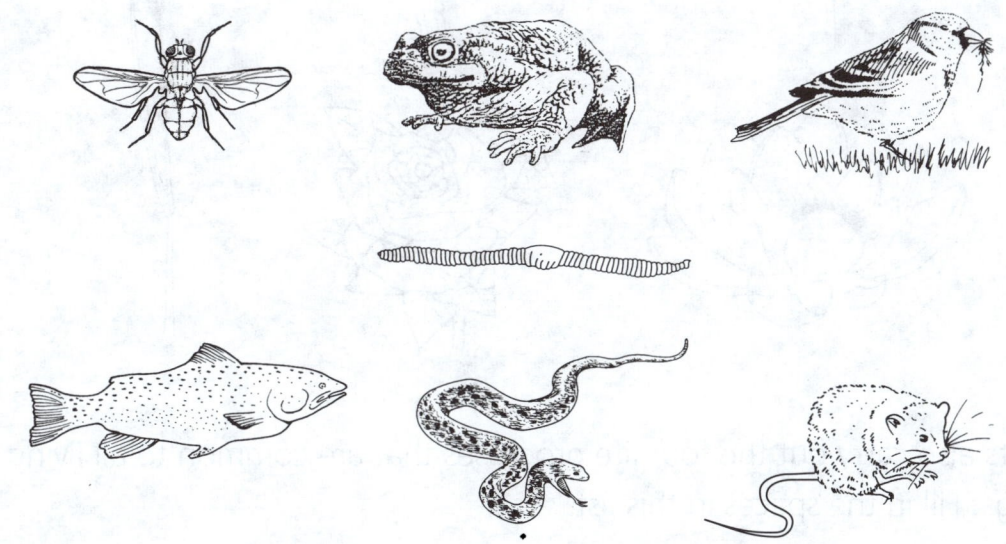

All living things need to take in food. They can all move in one way or another. They grow and produce offspring of their own species.

Write *yes* in the table below by the side of *four* life processes that are common to all of the living things shown above. Write *no* by the side of those that are not common to all.

breathing	1	nutrition	3
flight	2	swimming	4

reproduction	5	sight	7
movement	6	growth	8

Answers can be found on page 42

Plants are living things.

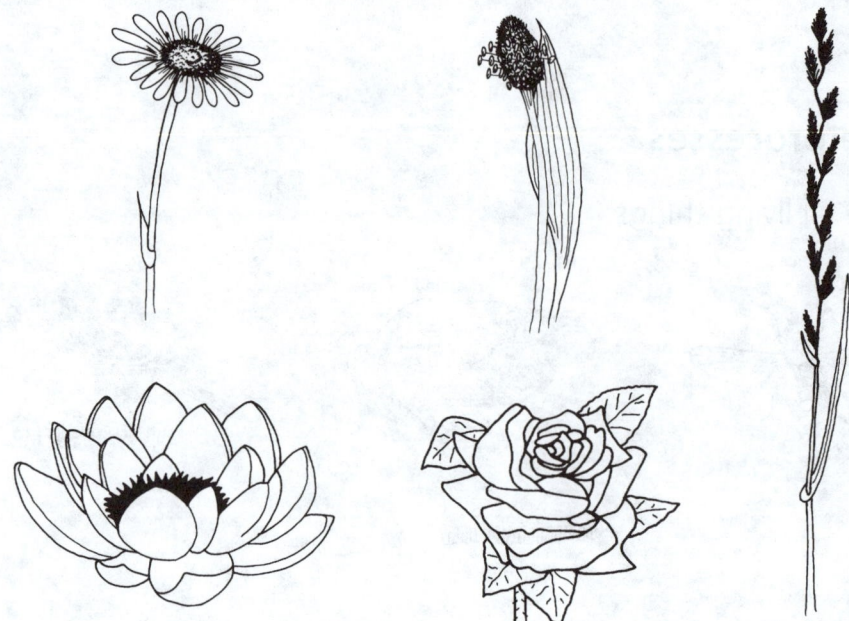

Plants also carry out the four life processes that are common to all living things. Fill in the spaces in this list.

- They begin their lives as a seed, and **9**_____ into a mature plant.
- When they are mature they **10**_____ to make copies of their species.
- They take in **11**_____ from the soil.
- They move towards light.

1.2 Variation and classification

Animals can be identified and sorted into groups by using a key.

The diagram at the top of the opposite page is a branch key. You answer *yes* or *no* to the questions about an animal to identify the group (e.g. **mammal**) to which it belongs.

Write the name of the group to which each of the animals in the table belong.

Answers can be found on page 42

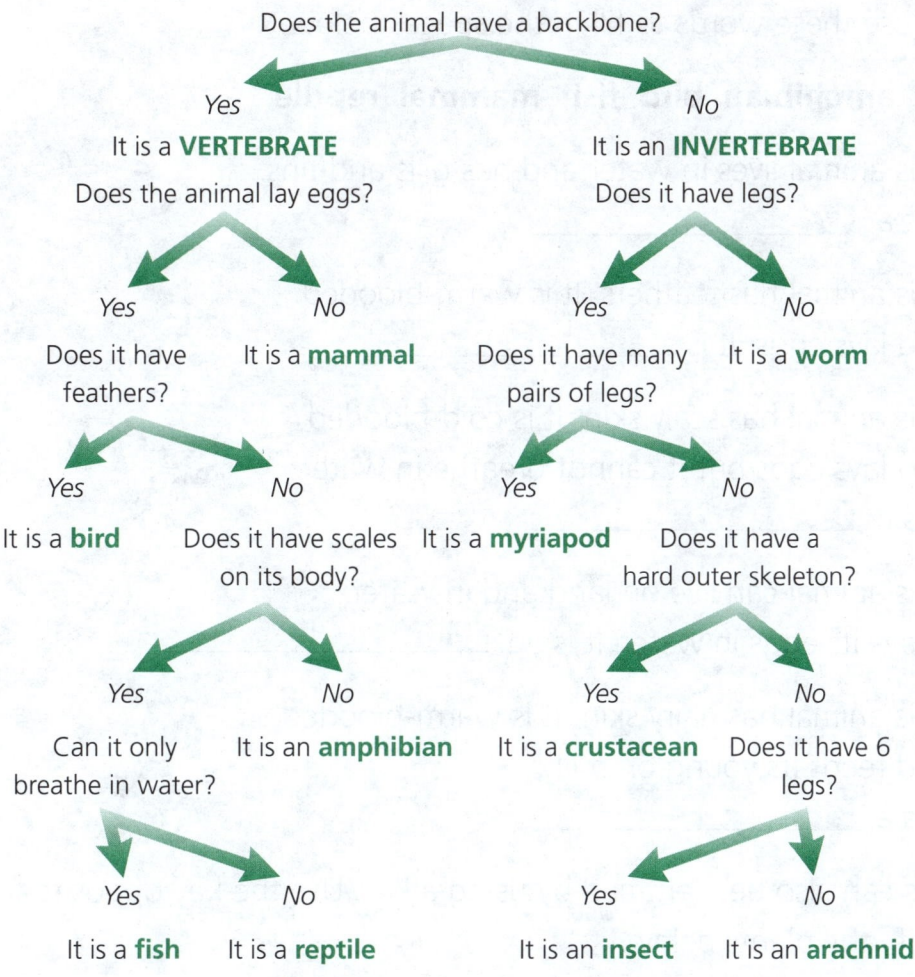

		Group
🐟	The trout is a	12 _____
🦀	The crab is a	13 _____
🐸	The toad is an	14 _____
🐛	The centipede is a	15 _____
🕷	The spider is an	16 _____

Answers can be found on page 42

Now use these words to fill in the spaces below:

amphibian bird fish mammal reptile

- This animal lives in water and has gills and fins. It is a `17` _____ .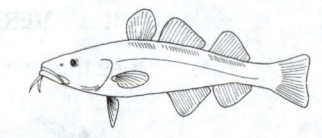

- This animal has feathers. It is warm-blooded and lays eggs. It is a `18` _____ .

- This animal has scaly skin. It is cold-blooded and lays eggs but it cannot breathe in water. It is a `19` _____ .

- This animal can live on land and in water. It lays its eggs in water. It is an `20` _____ .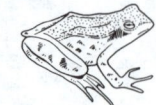

- This animal has hairy skin. It is warm-blooded and feeds its young on milk. It is a `21` _____ .

Plants can also be identified by using a key. Use the key opposite to identify the plants below.

A is a `22` _____ .

B is a `23` _____ .

C is a `24` _____ .

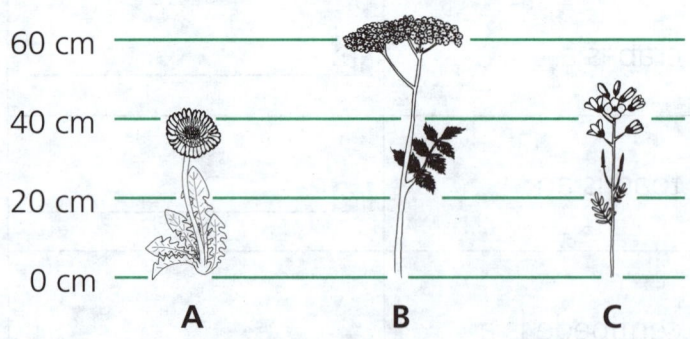

Answers can be found on page 42

	Grows under 15 cm	Grows between 15 cm and 60 cm	Grows over 60 cm	Flowers grow on single stem	Flower grows on branched stems	Grows in grassy places	Grows in weedy places	Grows among trees	4 petals on flower	5 petals on flower	Many petals on flower
buttercup		✓		✓		✓	✓			✓	
cuckoo flower		✓			✓	✓	✓				✓
dandelion		✓		✓		✓	✓				✓
daisy	✓			✓		✓				✓	
knapweed			✓	✓		✓	✓	✓			✓
cow parsley			✓		✓	✓	✓	✓	✓		

Humans as organisms

2.1 Nutrition

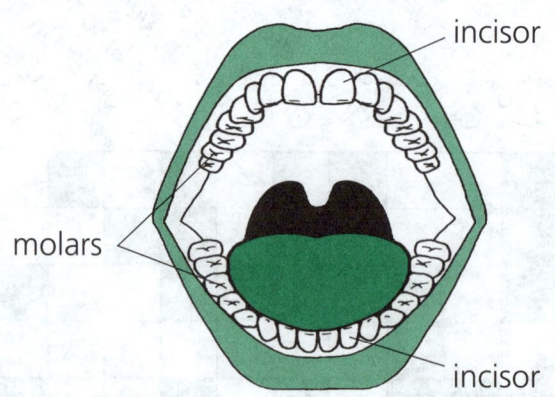

Babies do not need teeth because they do not eat solid food. During our lives we grow two sets of teeth. There are different teeth to perform different jobs. The **1**_____ cut the food into smaller chewable pieces. The **2**_____ grind food and crush it to make it easier to digest.

We need food to grow. We also need it to work our **3**_____ and the organs of the body such as the heart. Some foods keep us healthy. Those containing certain vitamins help to prevent us from catching diseases. Other foods help to keep our bowels clean. We need to eat different types of food. This gives us a **balanced diet**.

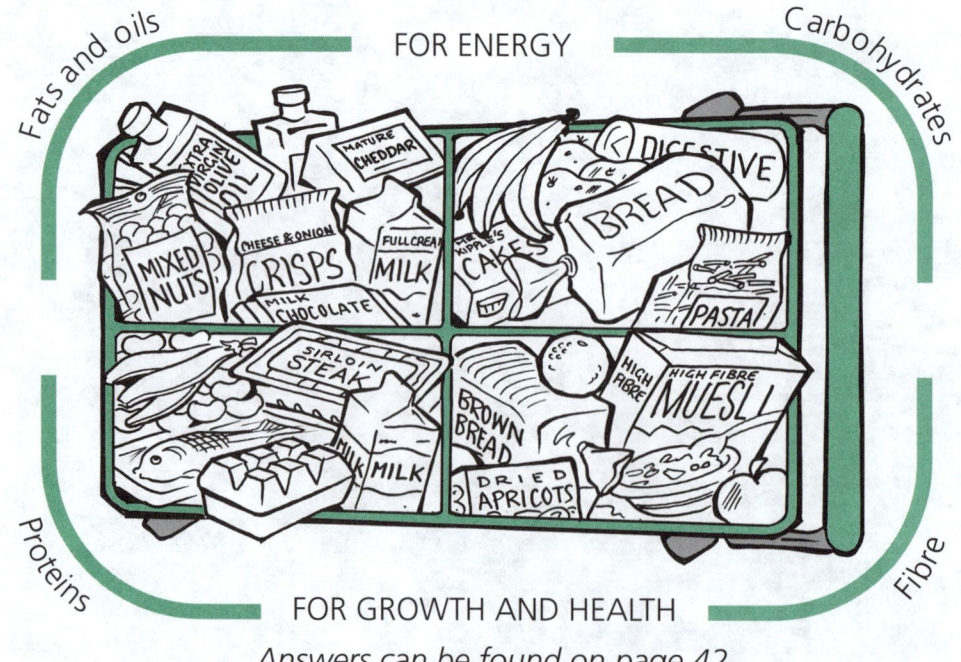

Answers can be found on page 42

Fill in the spaces in this chart.

Use	Group	Foods
for energy	fats	4 _____
for 5 _____	carbohydrates	bread, potatoes, bananas
for health	6 _____	fruit, cereals, dried fruit
for growth	7 _____	fish, milk, green beans

2.2 Circulation

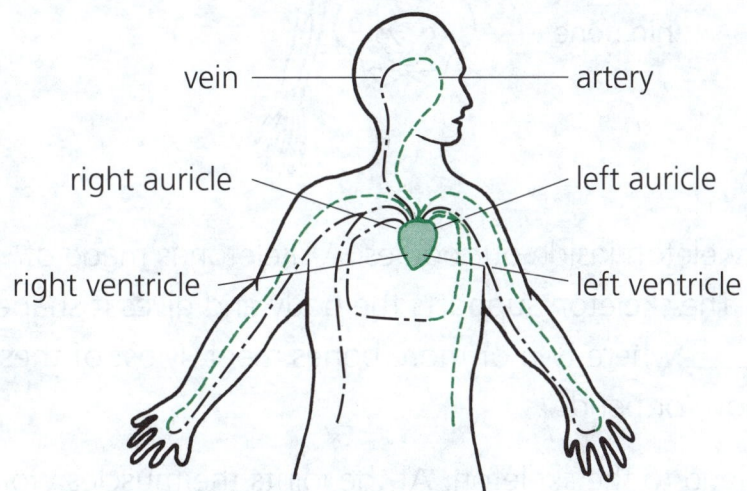

Your body is full of blood vessels. The 8 _____ pumps blood around the body through them. Blood is pumped out from the heart into **arteries**. It is carried back to the heart through the 9 _____. As the heart pumps blood into the arteries it causes a pulse. You can feel this by lightly pressing against the inside of your wrist.

Some children thought that their heart would beat faster when they exercised. They tested this and felt their 10 _____. Then they recorded their results in a table.

Activity	Heart beats per minute
resting	65
exercising	120

Answers can be found on page 42

Their results confirm that when you exercise your heart beats at a 11_____ rate than when you are resting.

2.3 Movement

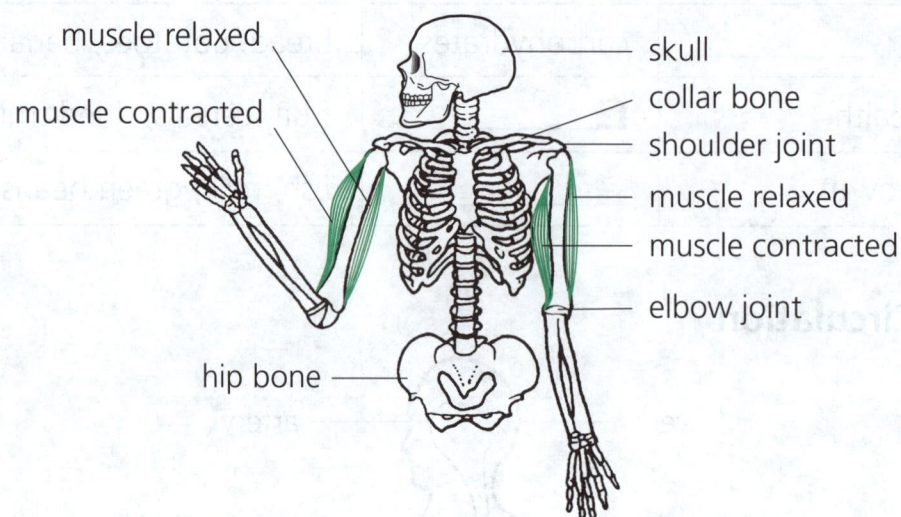

We all have a skeleton inside our bodies. A skeleton is made of 12_____. The skeleton supports the body and gives it shape. There is a 13_____ where two or more bones meet. Most of these help the body to move or bend.

Muscles are joined to the skeleton. At the joints the muscles work in pairs. One muscle 14_____ to make the joint bend. The other muscle contracts to straighten the joint.

2.4 Growth and reproduction

Humans start life as babies. They depend on their 15_____ for what they need. They could not survive without them. A baby gets its nutrients from 16_____. A baby develops into a toddler, then into

Answers can be found on page 42

a <u>**17**</u>_____. Children become <u>**18**</u>_____ when they are able to look after themselves and children of their own.

2.5 Health

Some people put things into their bodies that are not foods. These things do not help them to grow, give them energy or keep them healthy. They are used because people enjoy them or depend on them.

Smoking damages the lungs and heart. The <u>**19**</u>_____ in drinks affects the brain and causes people to make mistakes. People who drink a lot of alcohol can damage the organs in their body.

Some drugs are good for our bodies when we are ill. But people who take <u>**20**</u>_____ for enjoyment can be causing great damage to their bodies and minds.

Answers can be found on page 42

Green plants as organisms

3.1 Growth and nutrition

A plant is made up of different parts. Each part has a special job. Fill in the names of the parts on the diagram and in the table.

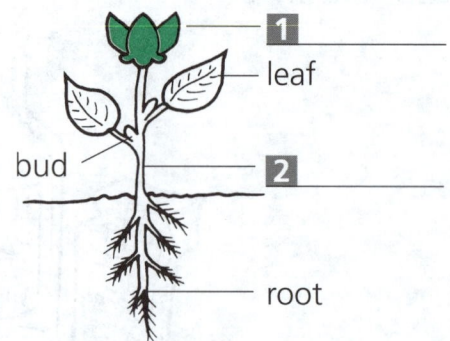

Part	Job
flower	contains the male and female parts of the plant; these make seeds
3 _____	make food for the plant; to do this they need sunlight, air, water and minerals
4 _____	hold the plant firmly in the soil
stem	supports the flower and leaves, and carries water and minerals up and down the plant
5 _____	are small partly grown leaves or flowers

This is a healthy, growing plant.

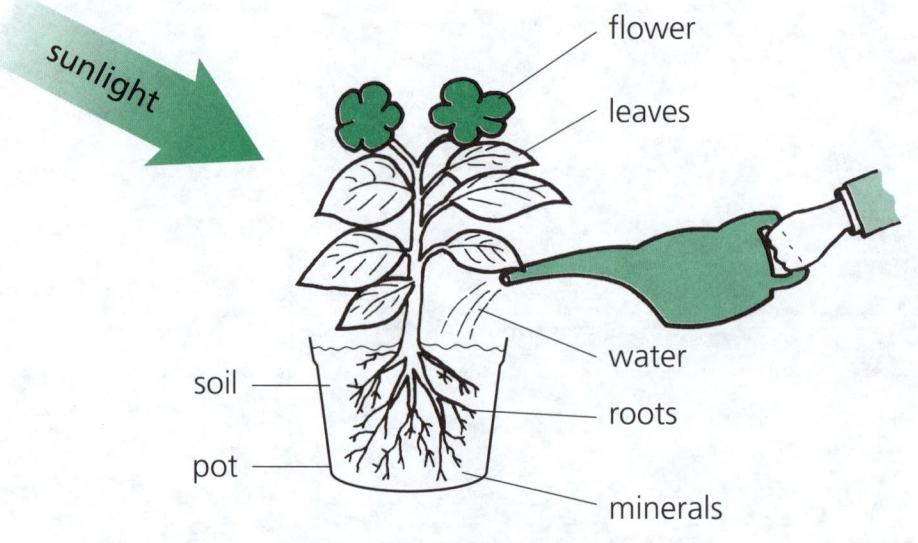

Answers can be found on page 42

To grow plants need **6**_____ and **minerals** which they take in through the roots. The leaves absorb **7**_____ which the plant needs to make food.

A plant is affected by the conditions that it grows in. If the leaves and stem are not a healthy colour, then the plant is not getting enough **8**_____. If the leaves and stem are not rigid but are soft and droop, then the roots are not absorbing enough **9**_____.

3.2 Reproduction

A flower is made up of different parts. Each part has a special job in the life-cycle of the plant. Fill in the names of the parts of a flower on the diagram and in the table.

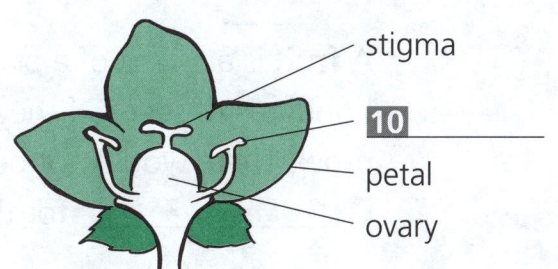

Part	Job
11_____	is the female part of the flower; pollen grains stick to it
12_____	are usually brightly coloured to attract insects to the flower
stamens	are the male parts of the flower; they are filled with grains of pollen
13_____	becomes a fruit after fertilization, containing the seeds

Answers can be found on page 42

wind

Seeds which will form new plants are made when pollen from the **stamen** is carried to the **stigma**. This can happen in one flower, or pollen can be carried from one flower to another. The pollen can be carried by 14_____ or by the 15_____.

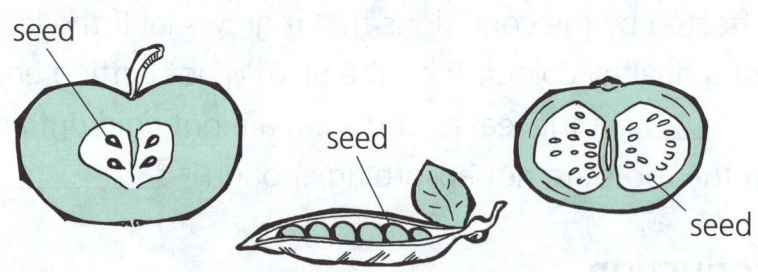

A **fruit** is any part of a plant that has 16_____. Many plants make hundreds of seeds. If they just fell close to the plant, not many would grow. There would not be enough sunlight, 17_____ or 18_____ for them all to grow.

Some plants have very light seeds or special 'wing' attachments so they can be carried far away from the parent plant by the 19_____.

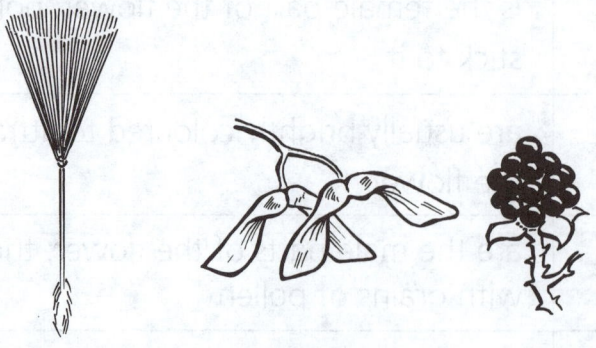

Answers can be found on page 42

Some fruits might be eaten by **20**_____ and the seeds deposited far away.

Seeds look dead, but if they have moist, warm conditions they will **germinate**. They have a food store which the tiny plant (**embryo**) inside uses when it grows.

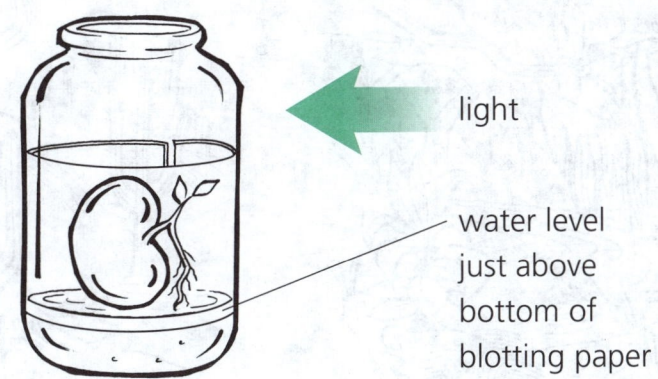

light

water level just above bottom of blotting paper

Answers can be found on page 42

Living things in their environment

4.1 Adaptation

A　　　　　　　　　　　　　　　　　　B

1 Tick *one* box that describes the climate in each picture.

Picture A   **Picture B**

Year-round sunshine ☐   Year-round sunshine ☐

Plenty of moisture ☐   Plenty of moisture ☐

2 In which picture would you find the most animals? Tick *one* box.

Picture A ☐   **Picture B** ☐

Why can many food chains begin in that environment?

3 _____

Now look at the picture below.

Answers can be found on page 42

How are the duck's feet suited to moving in deep water?

4 _____

How are the raven's feet suited to life in the tree branches?

5 _____

duck's foot

What makes the heron suited to moving in shallow water?

6 _____

The heron's feet are similar to the raven's feet. Both the raven and the heron could nest in the same place in the picture. Why couldn't the duck build its nest there?

raven's foot

7 _____

4.2 Feeding relationships

frog   grass snake   lettuce   slug

Complete this food chain involving the plant and animals above.

8 _____ → _____ → _____ → grass snake

- A **producer** is the first link in a food chain. It is often a green plant.
- A **consumer** is something that eats something.
- A **predator** is an animal that eats another animal.
- A **prey** is an animal that is eaten by a predator.

The producer in the food chain above is the **9** _____.

The consumer that is not a predator is the **10** _____.

The **11** _____ is a predator but not a prey.

The **12** _____ is a predator and also a prey.

Answers can be found on page 42

4.3 Micro-organisms

Use these words to fill in the spaces below.

warms   food   nutrients   oxygen   moist   organic   decays

Gardeners often build compost heaps from **13**_____ scraps and garden waste. You can make compost from most **14**_____ materials. A good compost heap encourages beneficial microbes and fungi to multiply so that the heap **15**_____ quickly. It is important to turn the compost heap with a fork regularly so that air reaches the centre, because microbes need **16**_____ to live and breed. The compost heap needs to be kept damp because microbes like **17**_____ conditions. As the organic matter rots it **18**_____ up. Microbes flourish when they are warm. When the micro-organisms have done their work the compost looks like fluffy garden soil. All the odours have gone and the compost is full of **19**_____ to encourage garden plants to grow and be healthy.

When food is canned (put in tins) it is heated to kill microbes. The food often spends months or even years in a warm cupboard. Why don't the microbes breed to dangerous levels again?

20 _____

_____

Why do dried foods like cereals and lentils stay edible for so long?

21 _____

Why does putting food in a freezer keep it fresh for a long time?

22 _____

Answers can be found on page 42

Grouping and classifying materials

Using only the materials labelled on this house, fill in the spaces in the table below. You can put *more than one* material in many of the spaces.

Materials	Property
1	rigid
2	clear, can be seen through
3	opaque
4	weatherproof
5	easily shaped with tools
6	hard, but breaks easily (brittle)
7	mixes and pours easily, dries hard and strong

8 _____ is transparent. Give *two* reasons why we need part of most rooms to be made from a transparent material:

9 _____.

Answers can be found on page 42

10 Have the materials below been made by people, or do they occur naturally? Tick one box for each material.

	Made	Natural
wood	☐	☐
brick	☐	☐
glass	☐	☐
stone	☐	☐
sand	☐	☐
plastic	☐	☐
steel	☐	☐
wool	☐	☐

Which one of these rocks and soils:

loam   granite   clay   chalk   peat

is the hardest? **11** _____

is the softest? **12** _____

Which *four* materials below began as rocks and are found on beaches?

grit   peat   sand   pebbles   shingle

13 _____ _____ _____ _____

Look at the picture at the top of the opposite page. Fill in the spaces below using these words.

boiling point   zero   freezing point   water vapour   one hundred

Water does not always remain a liquid. If it falls below **14** _____ degrees it turns into ice. This temperature is called the **15** _____. If it reaches **16** _____ degrees it turns into the gas we call steam. This temperature is called the **17** _____. Steam is invisible. The white cloud that we see coming from a kettle spout is steam cooling down and forming into the tiny droplets of liquid we call **18** _____.

Answers can be found on page 42

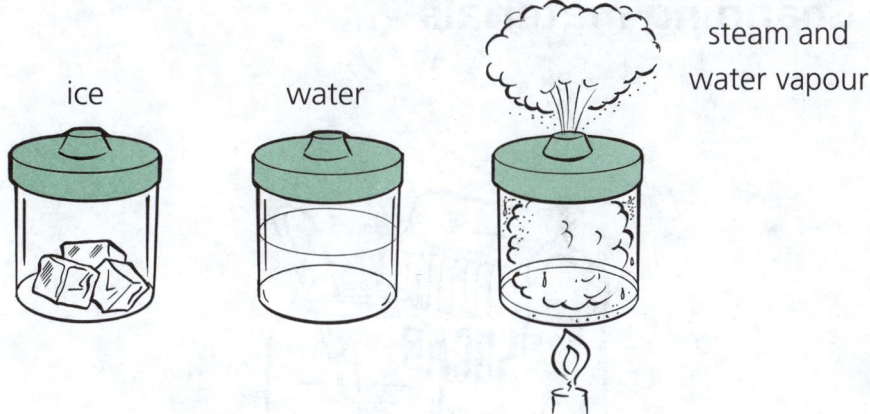

A *wooden* spoon has been left in a *metal* saucepan with a *plastic* handle. The saucepan contains *water* that has been heated to boiling point. Name *two* of these four materials that would be too hot to touch with a bare hand.

19 _____ _____

Why are hot water tanks in houses usually wrapped in thick material or foam?

20 _____

Tom is playing outside in the snow. Danny is inside waving at him. What is acting as a **thermal insulator** to keep the house warm despite the cold weather?

21 _____

Tom is wearing thick layers of clothes. These clothes act as thermal insulators so that Tom does not feel cold. How do these thermal insulators work?

22 _____

Answers can be found on page 42

Changing materials

Mixing materials can cause them to change. When you add add sugar to water, the sugar dissolves because it is a **soluble** material. The water is a **solute**. They combine to make a **solution**. Will any change take place when the materials in the table are mixed together? Answer *yes* or *no*.

salt and water	**1**	rice and lentils	**3**
grit and water	**2**	oil and water	**4**

soil and stones	**5**
coffee and water	**6**

Heating materials can also cause them to change. Use these words to fill the spaces in the list below.

evaporates ash hard melts burns

- If chocolate becomes warm it **7** _____.
- If water is boiled it **8** _____.
- If clay is heated it becomes **9** _____.
- If paper is heated it **10** _____ and turns to **11** _____.

Answers can be found on page 43

As materials are heated they get hotter. We use a **12**_____ to measure how hot they are. When we do this we record the **13**_____ in degrees **Celsius** (°C).

This graph shows what happened to the temperature of a pan of water that was heated and then left in a room to cool. The room temperature was 30 °C.

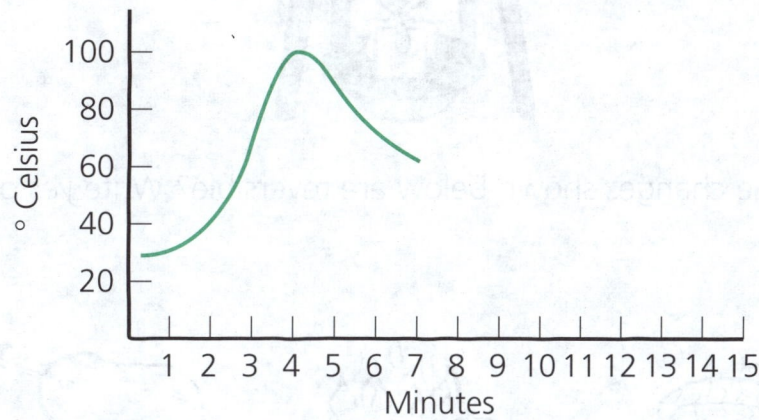

What was the hottest temperature of the water? **14**_____

What happened after 4 minutes? **15**_____

_____

What do you think the temperature of the water will be after 15 minutes? **16**_____

When some materials are changed the change can be reversed. Chocolate melts and becomes **liquid** when it is heated. When it cools it hardens and becomes **17**_____. This is a **reversible** change. When clay is heated it becomes hard and brittle. When it cools it does not become soft and plastic again. This is a change that *cannot* be reversed.

A number of reversible changes take place in the water cycle. Complete the labelling on the model of a simple water cycle shown at the top of the next page.

Answers can be found on page 43

TOPIC 6

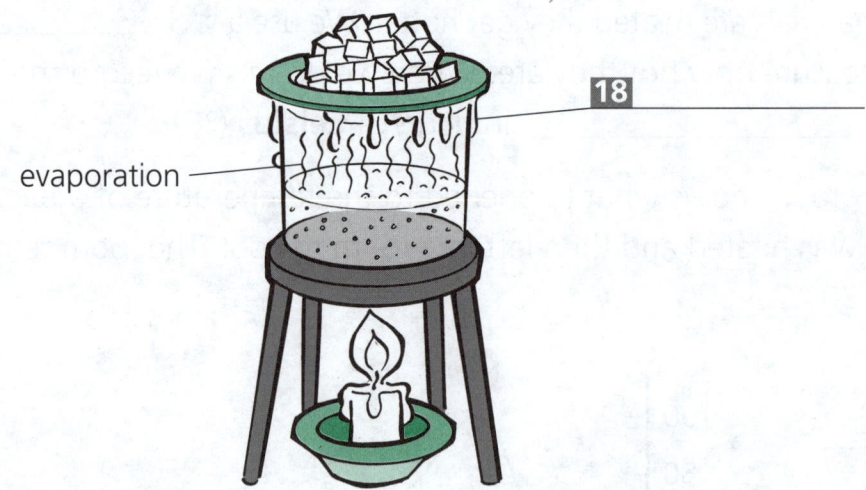

evaporation

18 _____

Which of the changes shown below are reversible? Write *yes* or *no* in the table.

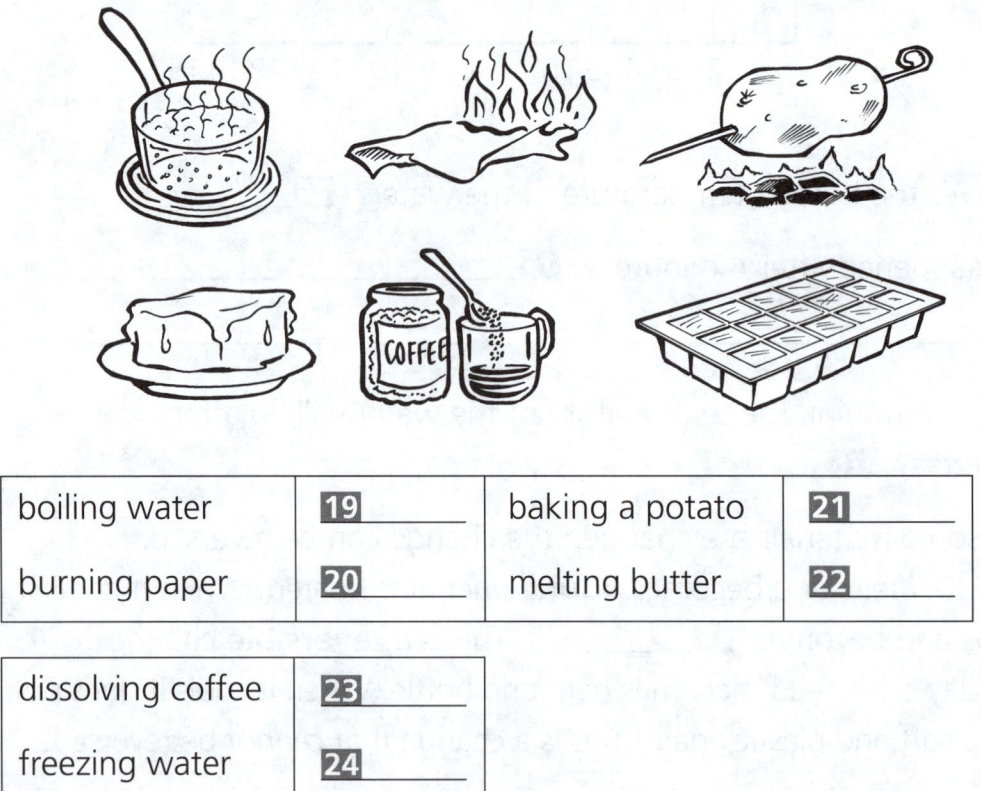

| boiling water | 19 _____ | baking a potato | 21 _____ |
| burning paper | 20 _____ | melting butter | 22 _____ |

| dissolving coffee | 23 _____ |
| freezing water | 24 _____ |

In what way(s) can the materials in the table opposite be changed? Tick the boxes and write R if the change is reversible.

Answers can be found on page 43

	dissolving	melting	boiling	condensing	freezing	evaporating	burning
25 chocolate							
26 salt							
27 moist air							
28 paper							
29 metal							
30 coal							
31 wood							
32 water							

Note that changes caused by burning are not reversible.

Answers can be found on page 43

Separating mixtures of materials

At a quarry diggers can lift out 500 kg or more material at a time. This material is often made up of many different particles. These are used for different purposes and need to be separated by sieving.

1 Match up the material to the sieve that separates it and holds it back:

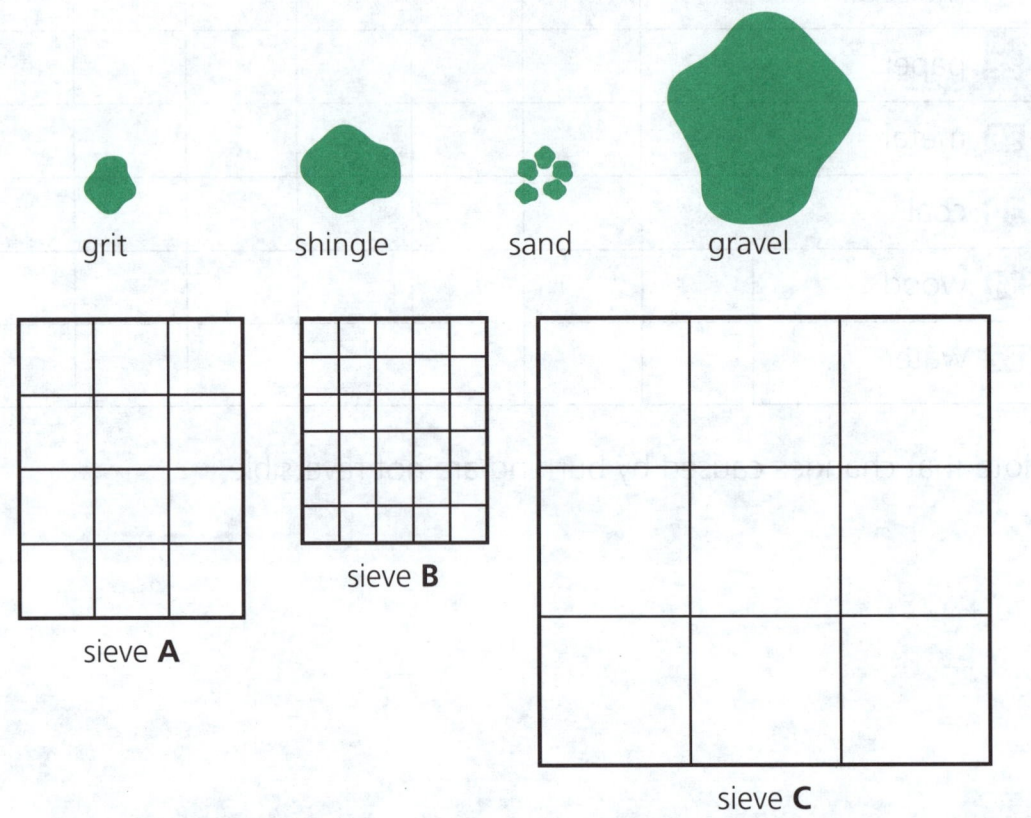

Which material is not caught and separated out by any sieve, and falls to the bottom? **2** _____

Now use these words to fill in the spaces below.

solute   solution   solid   soluble   dissolved   insoluble

If a **3** _____ disappears when it is mixed with water, then we say it has **4** _____. When this happens a **5** _____ is formed. A solid that will dissolve is said to be **6** _____. The liquid that makes it dissolve is called the **solvent** or the **7** _____. A solid that will not dissolve is called **8** _____.

Answers can be found on page 43

This is a bottle of sandy sea water. Sea water is salty. Brine is the name given to salty water.

The funnel contains a cone of filter paper. If the sandy sea water is poured into the funnel a clear solution of brine pours into the jar. Why does this happen?

9 _____

_____

What is the process that would leave *solids* of salt and other minerals in the jar? **10** _____

Putting the brine into a wide, open-topped container would speed up the process. How else could you speed up the process of obtaining the dissolved solids of salt and other minerals from the sea water? **11** _____

Some children carried out an investigation into dissolving solids in water. They wanted to test two hypotheses:

Hypothesis One *All soluble solids dissolve in water in equal amounts.*
Hypothesis Two *Hot water can dissolve more solids than cold water.*

They tested how many spoonsful of salt and sugar could be dissolved in 100 ml of water. Try this experiment yourself, write the results in the table below and then answer the questions.

	Spoonsful dissolved	
Soluble solid	in cool water	in hot water
Salt		
Sugar		

12 Hypothesis One is (tick the box):

true ☐   false ☐

What evidence shows this? **13** _____

Answers can be found on page 43

14 Hypothesis Two is (tick the box):

true ☐   false ☐

What evidence shows this?

15 _____

Into a jar of cool water has been tipped a spoonful of coffee granules and an egg cup each of uncooked rice and cooking oil. A lid has been put on the jar and it has been shaken and then left for a while.

In the middle of jar is a large band of brown liquid. Which two materials have combined to make this?

16 _____

Which material was the solute? **17** _____

Which material has been dissolved? **18** _____

Above the brown liquid there is a thin clear layer. What is it?

19 _____

Why is this clear liquid floating on top of the brown liquid?

20 _____

What is lying on the bottom of the jar? **21** _____

Why is it lying on the bottom?

22 _____

If the mixture in the jar was tipped into a saucepan and boiled for about ten minutes there would be far less water left in the saucepan than there was at the beginning. Give *two* reasons why there is less water.

23 _____

Answers can be found on page 43

Electricity

We need to make a complete circuit to make electrical devices work.

1 Put a tick in the box next to a picture if you think the bulb will light.

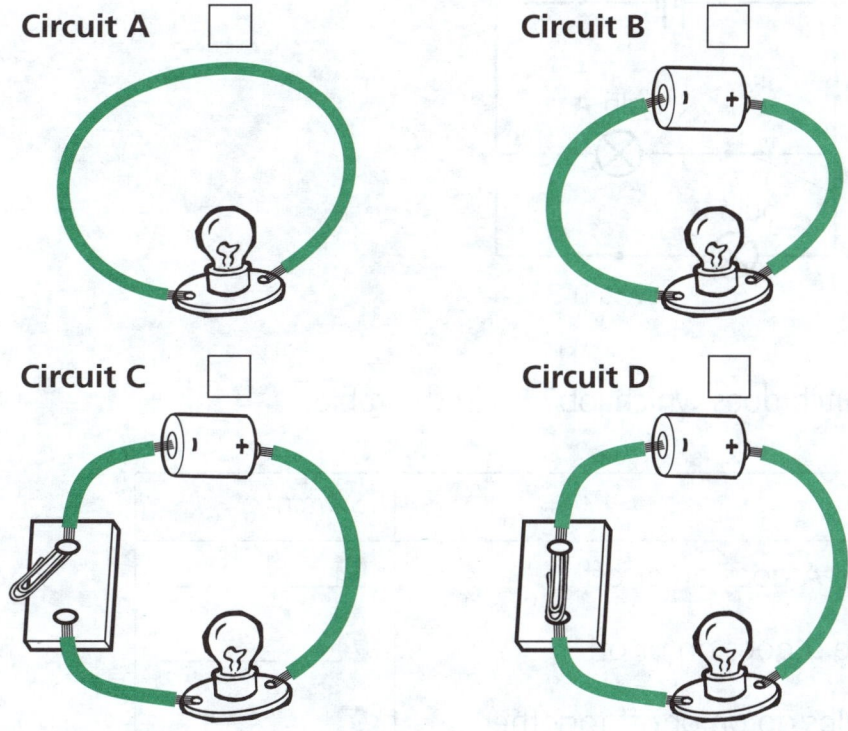

Match up the circuit diagrams below to the pictures of circuits above. Label each with the correct letter.

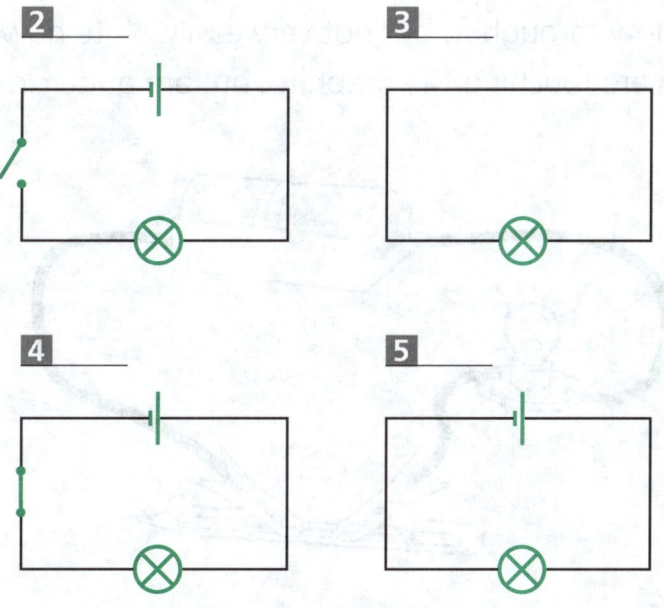

Answers can be found on page 43

Note there are two symbols you can use for a lamp.

This is the usual one.

But you will also come across this one.

The circuit below is called a **parallel circuit.**

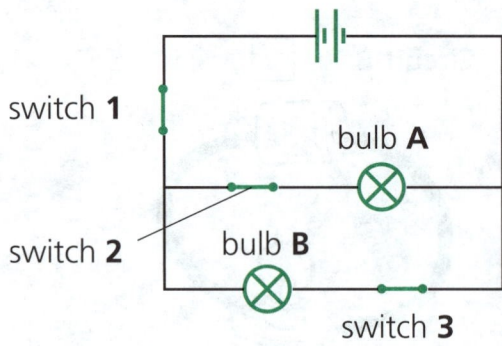

Which switch does which job? Fill in the table.

Job	Switch
only bulb **A** goes on or off	6
only bulb **B** goes on or off	7
both bulbs go on or off together	8

The 'lead' in a pencil is really a material called graphite. This allows electricity to flow through it, but not very easily. Note how these crocodile clips are touching the graphite, but are quite close together.

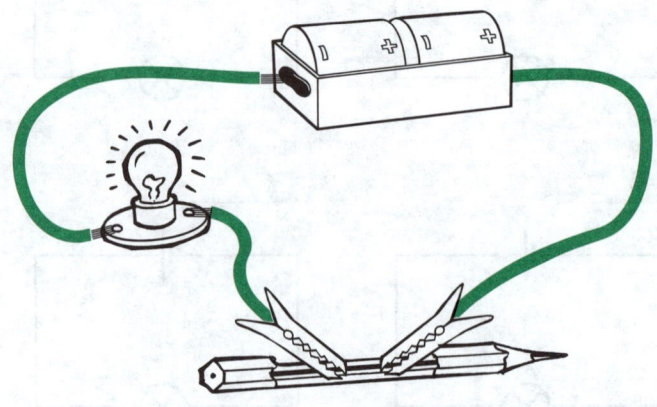

Answers can be found on page 43

9 When the crocodile clips are moved further apart the bulb becomes (tick one box):

brighter ☐   dimmer ☐

10 What do you call something that reduces the current in a circuit? (Tick *one* box.)

terminal ☐   cell ☐   conductor ☐   resistor ☐   insulator ☐

Asfa and Debbie are testing materials in two ways. Asfa uses different materials to complete a simple circuit. If the material conducts electricity it will light a bulb. When this test is finished Asfa gives the material to Debbie, who tests whether or not it is attracted by a magnet.

What results do you think Asfa and Debbie will get? Write *yes* or *no* in each space in the table.

Material	Bulb lights	Attracted by magnet
11 steel		
12 wood		
13 plastic		
14 copper		
15 aluminium		
16 silver		
17 paper		
18 glass		
19 gold		
20 brass		
21 wool		
22 stone		
23 iron		
24 lead		
25 rubber		

Answers can be found on page 43

TOPIC 8

Which of the materials in the table on the previous page are **electrical conductors**?

26 _____

_____

What name do we give the other materials in the table?

27 _____

All the electrical conductors in the table are **28** _____.
Are all metals attracted by magnets? **29** _____

Answers can be found on page 43

Forces and motion

9.1 Types of force

A magnet has two poles, a **1**_____ pole and a **2**_____ pole. If two magnets are placed with their poles close to one another, they exert a **force** on one another. If the poles are the same they repel each other. If the poles are different they **3**_____ each other.

Magnets attract iron and steel, which are metals.

Gravity is a force that pulls objects down.

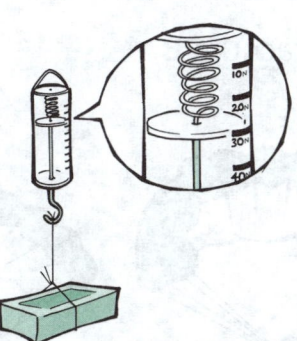

4_____ is pulling down on the brick. This down-force acts on the spring in the forcemeter and **5**_____ it. The scale on the forcemeter measures this force. **Weight** is the name for this force due to gravity. The forcemeter measures the weight of the brick in **newtons** (N). This brick weighs **6**____ N.

Friction is a force that slows objects down. Air resistance is a form of friction that can slow down a falling object.

Answers can be found on page 43

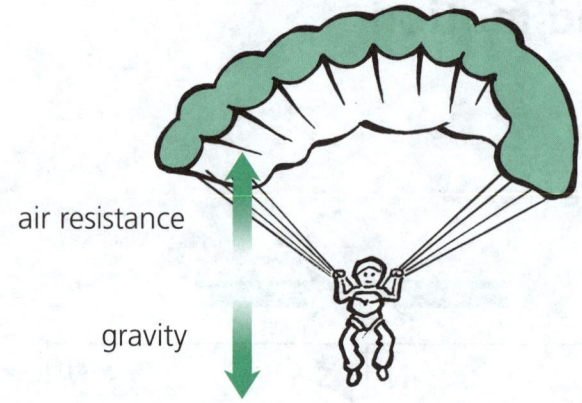

Friction between surfaces moving across another causes grip.

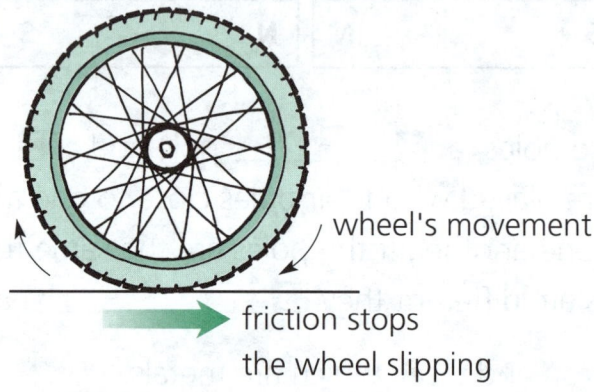

7 Which of these parachutes will fall more slowly to the ground?

parachute **A** ☐   parachute **B** ☐

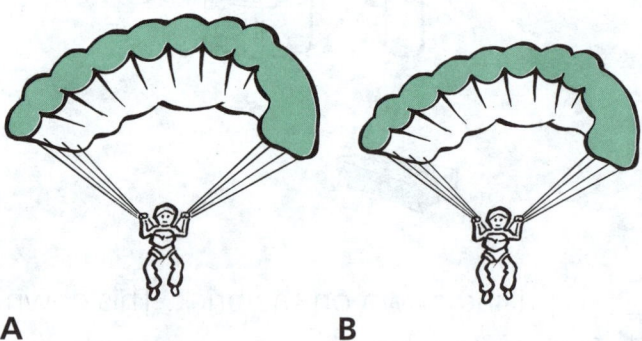

A   B

8 Which of these tyres will create the greater friction and give the better grip?

tyre **A** ☐   tyre **B** ☐

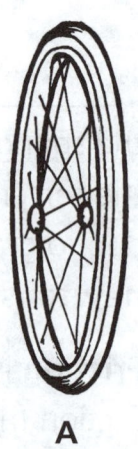 

A   B

Answers can be found on page 43

These athletes are using springs to exercise.

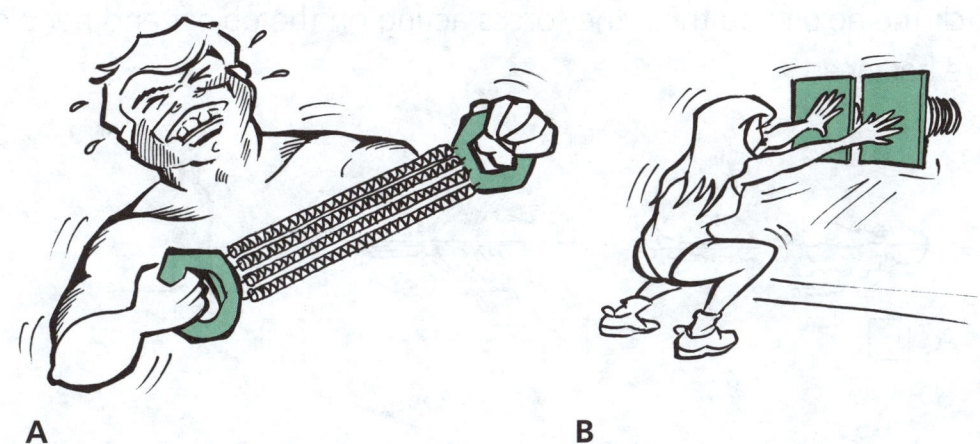

A   B

Athlete **A** is stretching a spring. This creates a 9_____ which pulls in on the athlete's arms.

Athlete **B** is 10_____ springs. This creates a force which pushes back on the athlete's arms.

A force is a push or a pull. Forces can act in different directions. Gravity is a 11_____-force. Draw an arrow to show the direction of each of these forces:

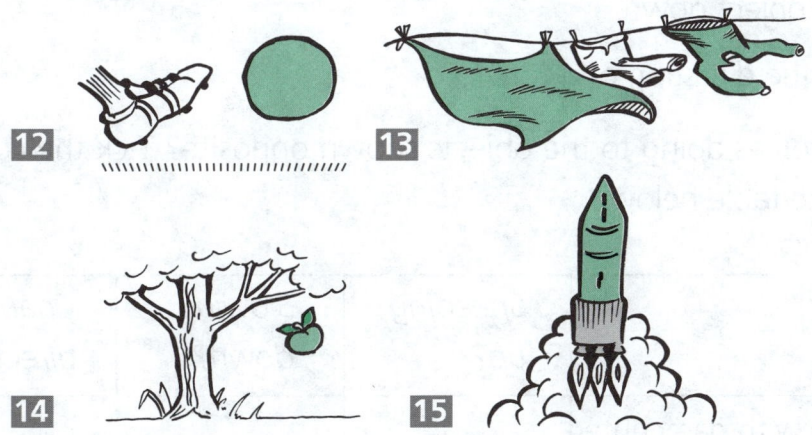

9.2 Balanced and unbalanced forces

When objects are not moving the 16_____ acting on them are **balanced**. For example, the up-force is equal to the down-force. When objects begin to move or speed up then one of the forces acting on them is 17_____ than the other. The forces are unbalanced.

Answers can be found on page 43

Which of the objects below have balanced forces acting on them?

18 Tick the box if you think the forces acting on the object and people are balanced.

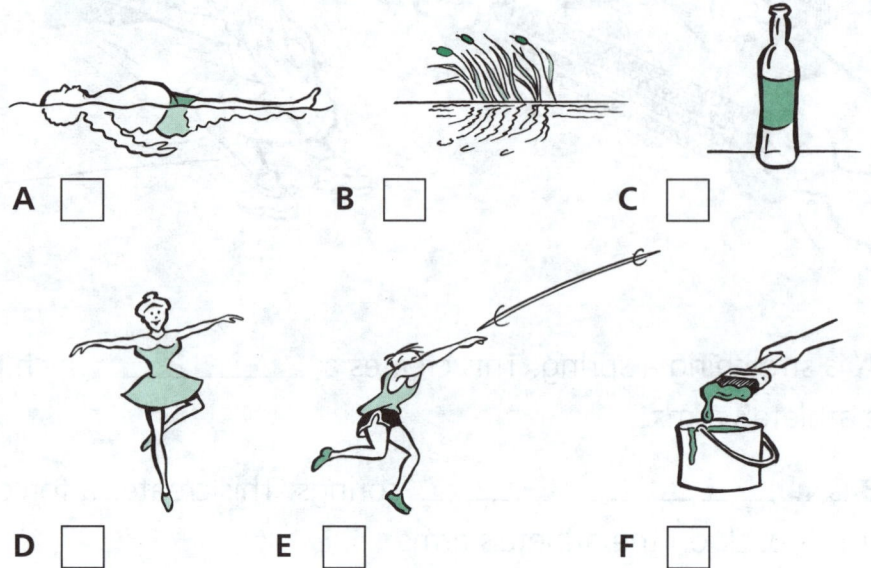

A ☐   B ☐   C ☐

D ☐   E ☐   F ☐

Objects are moved by forces that act upon them. Forces can:

- speed an object up
- slow an object down
- change the direction of a force

What are forces doing to the objects shown opposite? Tick the correct space in the table below.

Object	Speeding up?	Slowing down?	Changing direction?
19 plane with parachute			
20 sailing boat			
21 tennis ball			
22 roller-coaster car			

Answers can be found on page 43

9.3 The solar system

Use these words and numbers to fill in the spaces in the passage below.

**crescent   towards   9   solar system   orbits   year
seasons   28   daytime   fiery   24   reflects**

The Sun is at the centre of our **23**_____. Around the Sun **24**___ planets move in almost circular **25**_____. The further the planet is from the Sun, the longer the time the planet takes to complete one orbit. Our Earth completes its orbit in one **26**_____.

Our **27**_____ change as the Earth travels around the Sun, because the Earth tilts. In our summer the northern half of the Earth leans **28**_____ the Sun, while the southern half is in winter.

Every **29**____ hours the Earth spins around on its own axis. When the place on the Earth where you live is facing the Sun it is **30**_____, and when it is facing away from the Sun it is night.

Some nights we receive a little light from our Moon. The Moon is not a **31**_____ ball like the Sun. Its silvery grey surface softly **32**_____ some of the Sun's light onto the dark side of the Earth. As the Moon orbits the Earth it seem to change shape. As nights pass it grows from a thin **33**_____ shape to a fatter crescent shape, until it appears as full circle. Then it gets thinner again. This takes **34**____ nights. This is the time it takes the Moon to complete its journey around the Earth.

Answers can be found on page 43

Light and sound

10.1 Everyday effects of light

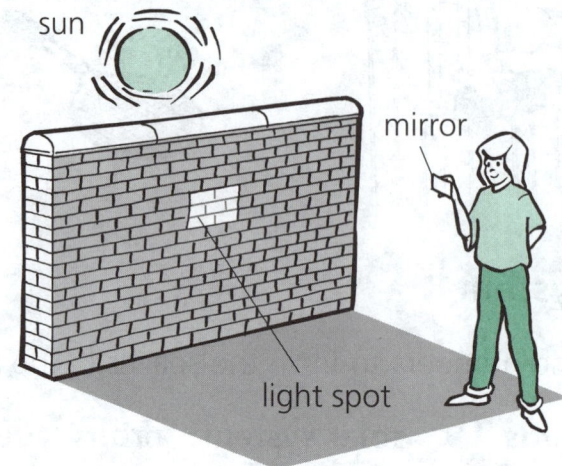

This side of the wall is in deep shadow, but there is a patch of bright light shining on it. How did it get there?

1 _____

Choose the correct word to fill in each of the spaces below.

translucent   transparent   opaque

Daniel wants to trace a picture from a book. At first he picks up an ordinary sheet of white paper and places it on the picture, but he cannot see the outline through it. This is because the paper is **2**_____. Next he picks up a piece of clear plastic. He can see the picture perfectly because this is **3**_____, but he does not have the special pens he needs to write on the shiny plastic. Next he picks up a piece of tracing paper. This works well. He can draw on it with an ordinary pencil and he can see the outline of the picture because the tracing paper is **4**_____.

Match up the same three words to their meanings in the following table.

Answers can be found on page 44

Word	Meaning
5 _____	allows no light to pass through
6 _____	allows some light to pass through
7 _____	allows almost all light to pass through

We are looking at a boy from above. *Look at his shadow.*
8 His shadow would look like this in:

the middle of the day ☐

the late afternoon ☐ (Tick one box.)

Explain your choice – where would the Sun be if it is making a shadow that shape? 9 _____

10.2 Seeing

Light enters our eyes from sources like these:

Moon   Sun   candle   headlamps   mirror   gas fire   television   torch

Sort these different sources of light. Write them in the correct column of the table.

10 Light from flames	11 Reflected light	12 Electric light
_____	_____	_____
_____	_____	_____
_____	_____	_____

10.3 Vibration and sound

To play a drum loudly you must hit it:

13 gently ☐   hard ☐   (Tick one box.)

Answers can be found on page 44

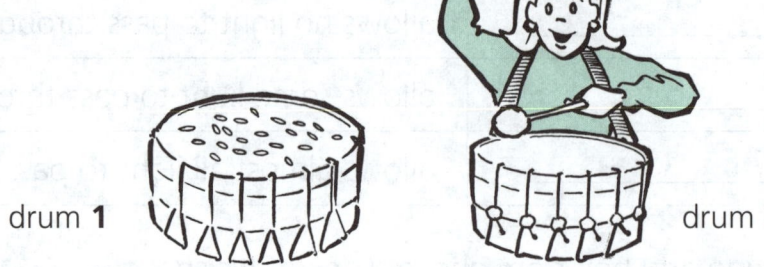

drum **1**   drum **2**

Rice grains are placed on drum **1**. Close by, drum **2** is played loudly. Each time drum **2** is hit the rice grains on drum **1** bounce in the air. No one touches drum **1**. Why do the rice grains bounce?

14 _____

_____

How does this experiment help to explain how human ears hear sound?

15 _____

_____

These instruments are identical in everything but size.

16 The main reason that the instruments are made in different sizes is:

to make the notes higher or lower in pitch ☐

to make louder or quieter sounds ☐   (Tick one box.)

Answers can be found on page 44

There are six pegs on a guitar that are used to make the strings tighter or slacker. This changes the **pitch** of the note that is played. The pitch of the note gets higher if you make the strings

17 slacker ☐   tighter ☐   (Tick one box.)

The sound of the car engine travels through the air to reach the girl's ears. What other material must the sound vibrations pass through?

18 _____

Answers can be found on page 44

Answers to self-check questions

For some questions other answers might be acceptable – check with your teacher.

Topic 1 Life processes, variation and classification

1. no
2. no
3. yes
4. no
5. yes
6. yes
7. no
8. yes
9. grow
10. reproduce
11. nutrients
12. fish
13. crustacean
14. amphibian
15. myriapod
16. arachnid
17. fish
18. bird
19. reptile
20. amphibian
21. mammal
22. dandelion
23. cow parsley
24. cuckoo flower

Topic 2 Humans as organisms

1. incisors
2. molars
3. muscles
4. oil, dairy products, chocolate, crisps, nuts
5. energy
6. fibre
7. proteins
8. heart
9. veins
10. pulse
11. faster
12. bones
13. joint
14. contracts
15. parents
16. milk
17. child
18. adults
19. alcohol
20. drugs

Topic 3 Green plants as organisms

1. flower
2. stem
3. leaves
4. roots
5. buds
6. water
7. sunlight
8. sunlight
9. water
10. stamen
11. stigma
12. petals
13. ovary
14. insects
15. wind
16. seeds
17. water
18. minerals
19. wind
20. animals

Topic 4 Living things in the environment

1. picture A – plenty of moisture; picture B – year-round sunshine
2. picture A
3. most food chains begin with green plants
4. webbed feet give more power for swimming
5. flexible toes and claws can grip around branches
6. it has long legs
7. ducks' feet can't grip around branches
8. lettuce → slug → frog → grass snake
9. lettuce
10. slug
11. grass snake
12. frog
13. food
14. organic
15. decays
16. oxygen
17. moist
18. warms
19. nutrients
20. cans are sealed so there is no contact with microbes outside; there is no oxygen for any microbes remaining inside
21. there is no moisture so microbes cannot survive
22. it is too cold for microbes to reproduce

Topic 5 Grouping and classifying materials

1. brick, wood, concrete
2. glass
3. brick, wood, concrete
4. brick, wood, concrete, glass
5. wood
6. glass
7. concrete
8. glass
9. to let in light; to see out
10. wood – natural; brick – made; glass – made; stone – natural; sand – natural; plastic – made; steel – made; wool – natural
11. granite
12. peat
13. sand, grit, shingle, pebbles
14. zero
15. freezing point
16. one hundred
17. boiling point
18. water vapour
19. metal, water
20. to slow down the cooling of the water
21. glass, curtains
22. they trap the warmth of his body

ANSWERS

Topic 6 Changing materials
1. yes
2. no
3. no
4. yes
5. no
6. yes
7. melts
8. evaporates
9. hard
10. burns
11. ash
12. thermometer
13. temperature
14. 100 °C
15. the water boiled and the pan was removed from the heat (or the heat turned off)
16. 30 °C
17. solid
18. condensation
19. yes
20. no
21. no
22. yes
23. yes
24. yes
25. melting (R)
26. dissolving (R)
27. condensing (R)
28. burning
29. melting (R)
30. burning
31. burning
32. boiling (R), freezing (R), evaporating (R)

Topic 7 Separating mixtures of materials
1. grit – sieve B; shingle – sieve A; gravel – sieve C
2. sand
3. solid
4. dissolved
5. solution
6. soluble
7. solute
8. insoluble
9. the paper fibres are permeable – there are tiny holes that the water can pass through, but the holes are far smaller than the grains of sand so they are held back
10. evaporation
11. heating/boiling
12. false
13. less salt dissolved than sugar
14. true
15. more spoonsful of solids dissolved in the hot water
16. coffee and water
17. water
18. coffee granules
19. cooking oil
20. the cooking oil is lighter (less dense) than the coffee solution
21. rice
22. the rice is heavier (more dense) than the coffee solution
23. water is lost (evaporates) as steam; water is absorbed by the rice

Topic 8 Electricity
1. circuit B, circuit D
2. C
3. A
4. D
5. B
6. switch 2
7. switch 3
8. switch 1
9. dimmer
10. resistor
11. yes, yes
12. no, no
13. no, no
14. yes, no
15. yes, no
16. yes, no
17. no, no
18. no, no
19. yes, no
20. yes, no
21. no, no
22. no, no
23. yes, yes
24. yes, no
25. no, no
26. steel, copper, aluminium, silver, gold, brass, iron, lead
27. insulators
28. metals
29. no

Topic 9 Forces and motion
1. north
2. south
3. attract
4. gravity
5. stretches
6. 30
7. A
8. B
9. force
10. compressing/squashing
11. down
12. →
13. →
14. ↓
15. ↑
16. forces
17. greater
18. A, C, D
19. slowing down
20. speeding up
21. changing direction
22. changing direction
23. solar system
24. 9
25. orbits
26. year
27. seasons
28. towards
29. 24
30. daytime
31. fiery
32. reflects
33. crescent
34. 28

Topic 10 Light and sound

1. reflected off the mirror
2. opaque
3. transparent
4. translucent
5. opaque
6. translucent
7. transparent
8. the middle of the day
9. high overhead
10. Sun, candle, gas fire
11. Moon, mirror
12. headlamps, television, torch
13. hard
14. the vibration from drum 2 travels through the air and causes the skin of drum 1 to vibrate
15. it shows how invisible sound waves can travel through the air and make your ear drum vibrate
16. to make the notes higher or lower in pitch
17. tighter
18. glass

PART 2

Test practice papers

After working through Part 1, your child should try each of the two test practice papers that you will find in this Part of the book.

Taking the practice tests

Help your child to reconstruct the test conditions that they will experience in the actual test.

- Find a place at home which comfortable and where it is reasonably quiet.
- Make sure that your child has two sharpened pencils.
- You could have an alarm clock set to go off after 35 minutes. If your child does not finish in time, let them carry on until they do.

By timing yourself in this way, you and your child will become more aware of just how much time there is in the National Test itself.

Marking the questions

You should take responsibility for marking your child's practice tests. You will find the answers and a breakdown of the marks awarded on pages 68–73.

Instructions

1. Try to answer all the questions. You have 35 minutes to do each test.
2. Read the questions carefully.
3. Look out for the different 'command' words used in the questions. The most common words you are likely to meet in the tests are explained on the next page.
4. If you cannot answer a question, move on to the next one. If you have time, you can go back to the question later.
5. The lines and spaces give you a clue about how much you are expected to write for your answer.
6. When you have finished the tests, turn to the answers and mark scheme on pages 68–73. Fill in the mark boxes by the side of each question.
7. The marking grid and level chart on page 74 will help you to convert your score into your level of achievement.

Good luck!

Words of command used in the test questions

Complete

You finish the sentence.

Example

Q Complete this sentence 'Unbalanced forces can _____.'

A You would write *make an object move*.

Describe

You write down what you would do or what you would see in as much detail as possible.

Example

Q Describe what happened when the heat was turned off.

A The temperature of the water began to fall.

Explain

You give a reason for your answer.

Example

Q Explain how blood circulates.

A Blood is pumped out of the heart into arteries and returns to the heart in veins.

Give

You write down the answer.

Example

Q Give two reasons why animals have skeletons.

A A skeleton supports the body of an animal.
A skeleton protects the organs inside the body.

Write

You write down the answer. (See **Give** above.)

Test A

Q1

These plants do not look the same but they all have to do the same things to survive.
They all need to make food to stay alive.
Write down two other things that *all* plants do while they are alive.

a ....

b ....

2 Q1

Q2 Plants need roots.
Tick the *two* sentences that are true.

i   The roots make food for the plant. ☐

ii The roots of a plant take up water and
    nutrients from the soil. ☐

iii The roots of the plant turn the leaves green. ☐

iv The roots help the plant to reproduce. ☐

v   The roots can hold the plant firmly in the soil. ☐

2 Q2

Answers can be found on page 68

Q3 A black plastic bag is tied around one plant and a transparent plastic bag around another plant.

a Will they both grow well? ....

b Write a reason why. ....

....

Q4 The table shows the nutritional value of some foods.

Food	Protein/g	Carbohydrate/g	Fat/g	Fibre/g
celery	0	1.2	0	0.9
banana	1.3	15.2	0	1.9
chocolate bar	2.8	25.3	12.4	0.1
chevda (Bombay mix)	18.2	35.3	17.9	5.9
tube of peppermints	0	31.3	0	0
fruit yoghurt	6.1	12.3	5.9	2.8

a Write down the names of two of the foods that you should avoid eating too much of.

....

b Give your reason(s) for choosing these foods.

....

Answers can be found on pages 68–70

Q5

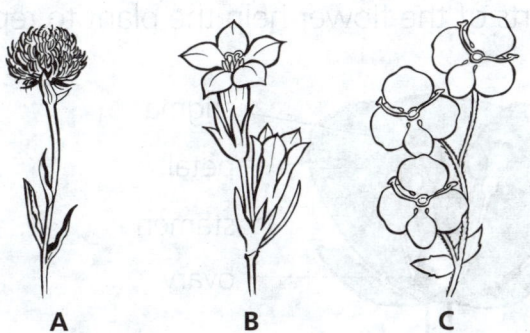

A   B   C

Use this key to identify the plants above.

Does the plant have a single main stem?

Yes — Does the flower have more than 5 petals?
No — Does the flower have less than 5 petals?

Yes — Is the flower shaped like a globe?
No — Is the flower bell-shaped?
Yes — **speedwell**
No — Are the edges of the leaf ragged?

Yes — **hawkbit**
No — **rampion**

Yes — **foxglove**
No — **gentian**

Yes — **sow thistle**
No — **forget-me-not**

A is a ....

B is a ....

C is a ....

Answers can be found on page 68–70

Q6 Explain how these parts of the flower help the plant to reproduce.

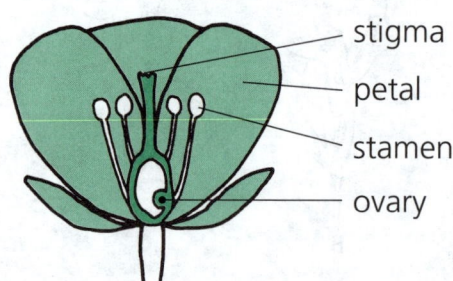

a   petal ....

....

b   stamen ....

....

c   stigma ....

....

d   ovary ....

....

Q7 Mohan exercised. This graph shows what happened to his pulse rate.

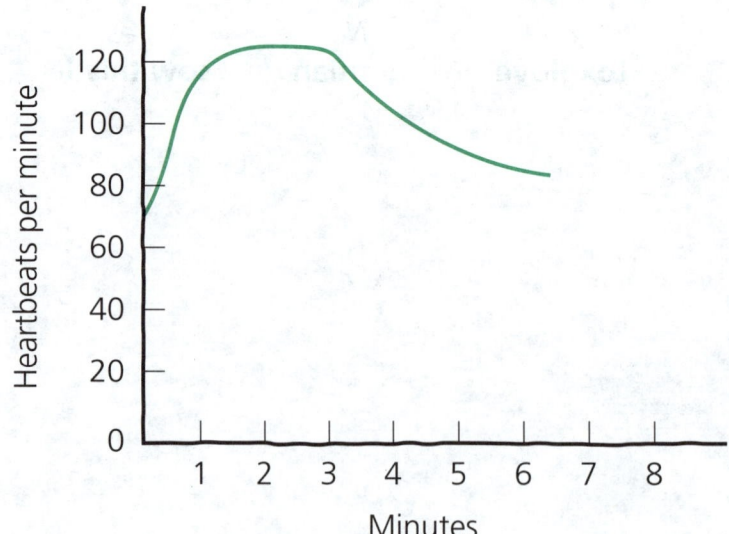

Answers can be found on pages 68–70

a For how long did Mohan exercise? ....

b Explain your answer. ....

....

Q8 Two containers of salty water were placed on a window sill in a sunny position. They were not moved for a few days.

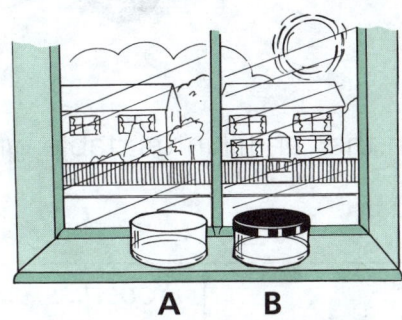

a Describe *two* changes that will occur in container A.

....

....

b Describe *two* changes that will occur in container B.

....

....

Q9

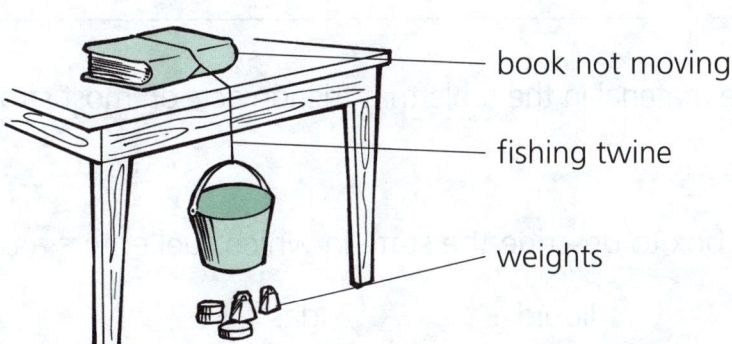

- book not moving
- fishing twine
- weights

a Name the *two* balanced forces that are acting on the book.

....

Answers can be found on pages 68–70

b Explain why the book will eventually move if weights are added to the bucket.

....

Q10

Using only the labels on the car, fill in the table with the correct materials (*one* per box).

Material	Properties
a	looks good and slips through the air easily
b	transparent and shatterproof
c	pressed into shape, but strong and rigid
d	flexible, absorbs bumps, strong grip

e Name the material in the table that friction acts on most strongly.

....

5
Q10

Q11 a Tick *one* box to describe the state in which fuel enters a car.

solid ☐   liquid ☐   gas ☐

b Tick *one* box which best describes the state in which fuel leaves a car.

solid ☐   liquid ☐   gas ☐

2
Q11

Answers can be found on pages 68–70

Q12 Gita and Michael were told that soils are often made from mixtures of different materials, such as clay, stones and organic materials. All soils are not alike. Clay is very sticky when wet. The more clay there is in a soil the better you can roll it into a sausage shape, then bend it into a ring without cracks appearing. The children wetted some different soils, then tried the 'rolling and bending into a ring' test.

They recorded their results in this table.

Wet soil	Rolled	Bent without cracking
peat	✗	✗
marl	✓	✓
sand	✗	✗
loam	✓	✗

a Which soil contained the most clay? ....

b Answer this by looking at the table. Is wet sand stickier than wet peat? (Tick *one* box.)

yes ☐   no ☐   can't tell ☐

c Explain your answer to part **b**.
....

d Name *one* wet soil that is less sticky than marl but more sticky than sand. ....

Q13 The following table shows some of the properties of solids, liquids and gases. Complete the table by ticking to show whether each property applies to a solid, a liquid or a gas.

The first row has been done for you. The other rows need only *one* tick each.

Answers can be found on pages 68–70

Property	Solid	Liquid	Gas
a can flow through a pipe easily		✓	✓
b changes its shape when poured from one container into a different container			
c keeps its own shape			
d can be shaped into structures			
e can be squashed into a much smaller volume			
f can expand into all parts of a sealed container			

Q13 — 5

Q14 a Tick *one* box to explain why electrical wires are made from copper.

Copper is

shiny ☐   a conductor ☐   magnetic ☐

b Tick *one* box to explain why electrical wires are covered in plastic.

Plastic is

easily melted ☐   not magnetic ☐   an insulator ☐

Q14 — 2

Q15 a Label the poles of these magnets by putting N, N, S, S in the correct places. The magnets are attracting each other.

b Why did you choose to label the magnets as you did?

....

Q15 — 2

Q16 a Josie has spilled a bag of flour into a box of Rice Crispies. What is the easiest way to separate the large Rice Crispie grains from the flour?

....

Answers can be found on pages 68–70

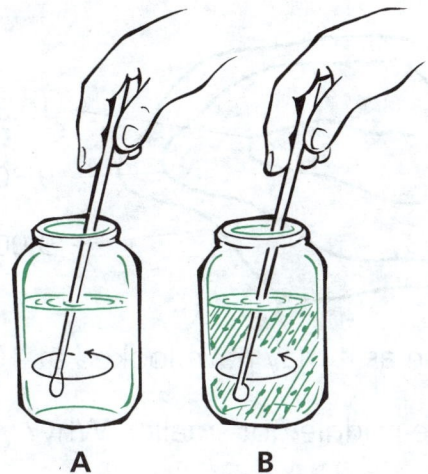

b Jar A contains a solution of sugar and water.
Jar B contains water and sand.

Jar B has just been stirred. What would be the quickest way to remove the grains of sand from the water?

....

c Jar A above is left without a lid in a warm room. After a few days all that remains in the jar is sugar.

What name do scientists give to this way of recovering solids from a solution? ....

d When the water left Jar A, it left as

solid ☐   liquid ☐   vapour ☐   gas ☐   (Tick *one* box.)

e Josie takes a small glass of water out of the fridge. She adds five teaspoons of sugar to the water. No matter how much she stirs some grains of sugar still remain in the water. Without adding any more water, how can she make all the sugar dissolve?

....

Q16

Q17 A litre of water was poured onto the playground to form a puddle. No water soaked into the playground. Every 30 minutes the outline of the puddle was recorded.

Answers can be found on pages 68–70

Day 1

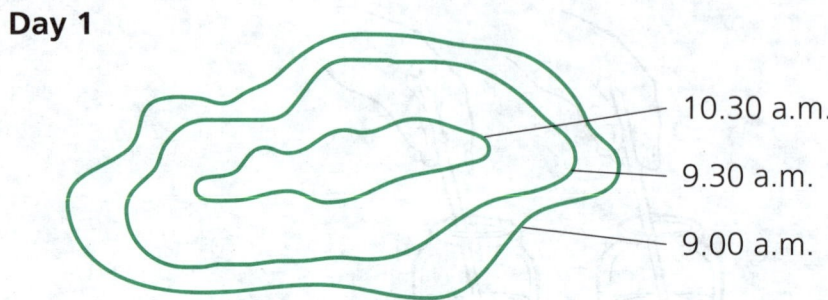

- 10.30 a.m.
- 9.30 a.m.
- 9.00 a.m.

a Draw in the outline as it may have looked at 10.00 am.

b As time passed the puddle got smaller. Why?

....

The next day the experiment was repeated. The same amount of water was placed in exactly the same place. Again the outline was recorded at half-hour intervals.

Day 2

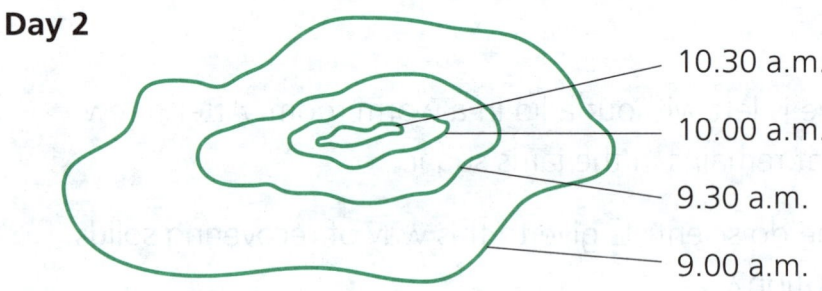

- 10.30 a.m.
- 10.00 a.m.
- 9.30 a.m.
- 9.00 a.m.

c Tick the day on which the weather was warmer.

Day 1 ☐   Day 2 ☐

d How do you know that one day was warmer than the other?

....

....

Q17 — 4

Q18 A cup of hot tea and glass of iced squash were left in the same room.

The graph on the opposite page shows the way the temperature of the drinks changed.

a Which line was the cup of tea, A or B? ....

b What was the temperature of the room that the drinks were left in? ....

Q18 — 2

Answers can be found on pages 68–70

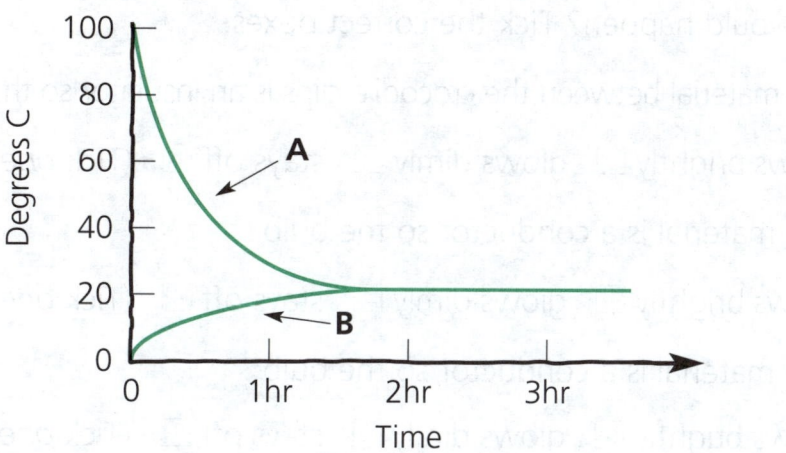

Q19 Look at these two series circuits.

Circuit 1 **Circuit 2**

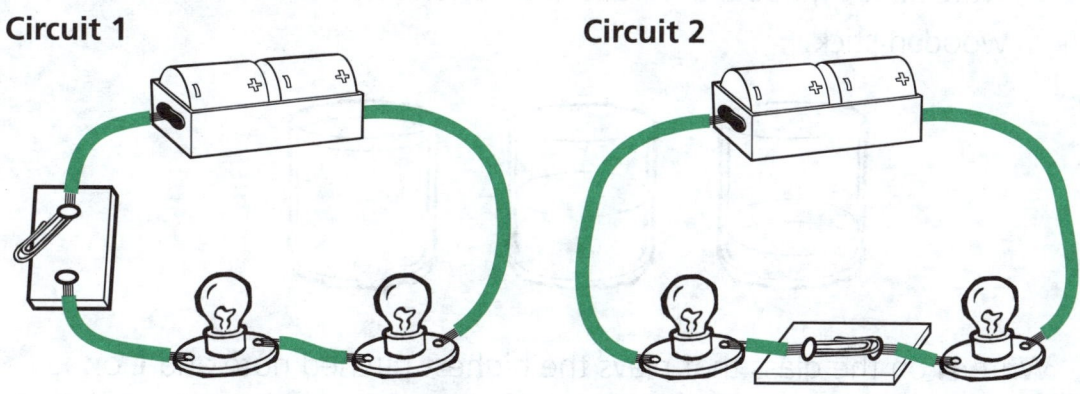

a Which one is switched on? ....

b If the switch in Circuit 2 was moved to the off position what would happen?

....

This circuit has been completed by connecting a strip of material between two crocodile clips.

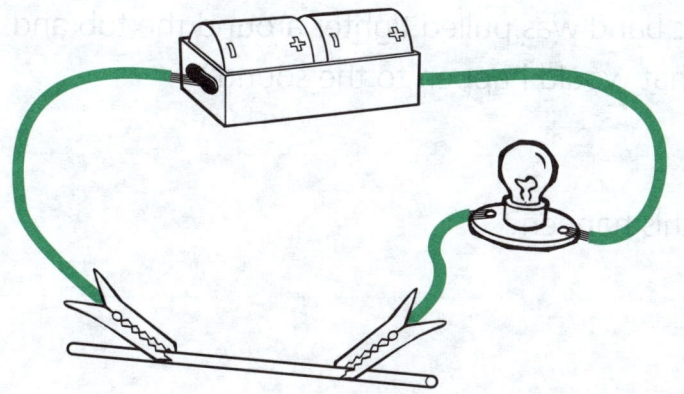

Answers can be found on pages 68–70

What would happen? Tick the correct boxes.

c The material between the crocodile clips is an insulator so the bulb

glows brightly ☐   glows dimly ☐   stays off ☐   (Tick *one* box.)

d The material is a conductor so the bulb

glows brightly ☐   glows dimly ☐   stays off ☐   (Tick *one* box.)

e The material is a conductor so the bulb

glows brightly ☐   glows dimly ☐   stays off ☐   (Tick *one* box.)

Q20 a These identical glasses are filled with different amounts of water. Each made a different note when struck with a wooden stick.

Write **H** on the glass that plays the highest pitched note and **L** on the glass that plays the lowest pitched note.

b This is an elastic band, being plucked by a child.

If the elastic band was pulled tighter around the tub and plucked, what would happen to the sound?

....

c Why does this happen?

....

Answers can be found on pages 68–70

Test B

Q1 Narrinder is planting two shrubs.

a Which one of them do you you think will grow better? ....

b Give a reason why. ....

....

Q2 Leaves are very important to a plant.

Tick the *two* statements that are true.

i Leaves make food from sunlight and air. ☐

ii Leaves make pollen. ☐

iii Leaves attract insects to the plant. ☐

iv Leaves help to disperse seeds. ☐

v Leaves release oxygen and moisture into the air. ☐

Q3 How do teeth help us to digest food?
Tick *two* boxes.

i They look attractive. ☐   ii Teeth make saliva. ☐

iii They taste the food. ☐   iv They break food into smaller pieces. ☐

v They crush and grind food. ☐   vi Teeth can decay. ☐

Answers can be found on pages 71–73

Q4 There are many blood vessels in the body that carry blood away from the heart to parts of the body.

Complete (you finish the sentence):

a These blood vessels are called ....

There are also blood vessels that bring blood back to the heart from all parts of the body.

Complete:

b These blood vessels are called ....

c The the heart is a pump that helps blood to ....

....

Q5 All vertebrates have internal skeletons.

Write down *two* reasons why vertebrate animals have internal skeletons. ....

....

Q6 Muscles often work in pairs. Parts of the skeleton are moved by one muscle expanding and its partner contracting.

muscle A
muscle B
muscle D
muscle C

a Write the letter of the muscle that contracts to bend the arm. ....

b Write the letter of the muscle that expands when the arm is bent. ....

Answers can be found on pages 71–73

Q7 This seed is beginning to germinate.

Tick those conditions that are necessary in order for it to germinate.

dryness ☐   moisture ☐   light ☐

warmth ☐   soil ☐   darkness ☐

Q8 Seeds are contained in fruits of different shapes and sizes. Explain how different designs of fruit give the seeds inside a chance to grow into plants.

a wings ....

b berries ....

c nuts ....

Q9

cooking oil   margarine   chocolate   paper

wood   metal   dough   stone

Write the name of *each* material in the correct box A, B or C overleaf.

Answers can be found on pages 71–73

Will it change when heated?

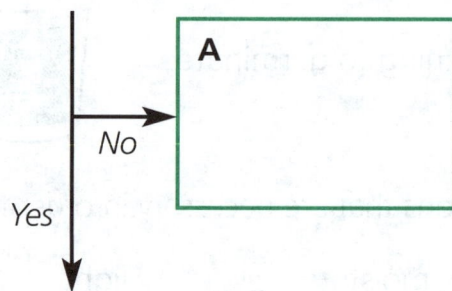

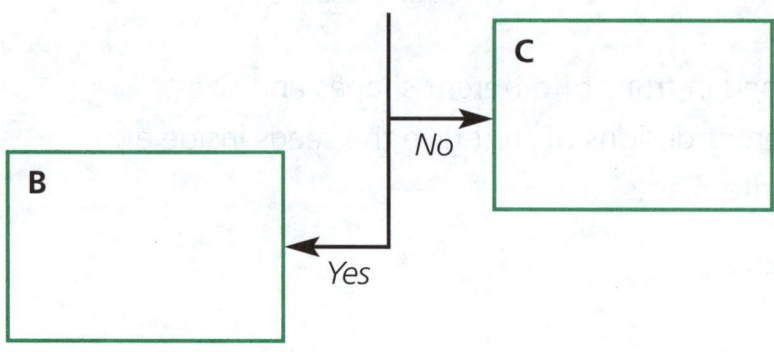

Can the change be reversed?

Q10 Which *two* statements best describe what is happening to the ball?

i The up-force and down-force are in balance. ☐

ii The up-force is greater than the down-force. ☐

iii The down-force is greater than the up-force. ☐

iv Gravity is acting on the ball. ☐

Q11 a What force is being measured by the forcemeter? (Tick *one* box.)

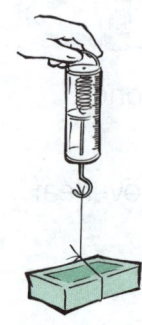

friction ☐

gravity ☐

air resistance ☐

centrifugal force ☐

Answers can be found on pages 71–73

b If the brick was hung in a bucket of water its weight would be less. Explain why.

....

....

Q12 a Draw an arrow to show the direction of the force that the trampoline is exerting on Lucy.

b Draw an arrow to show the direction of the force that Ben is exerting on the pirate.

Q13

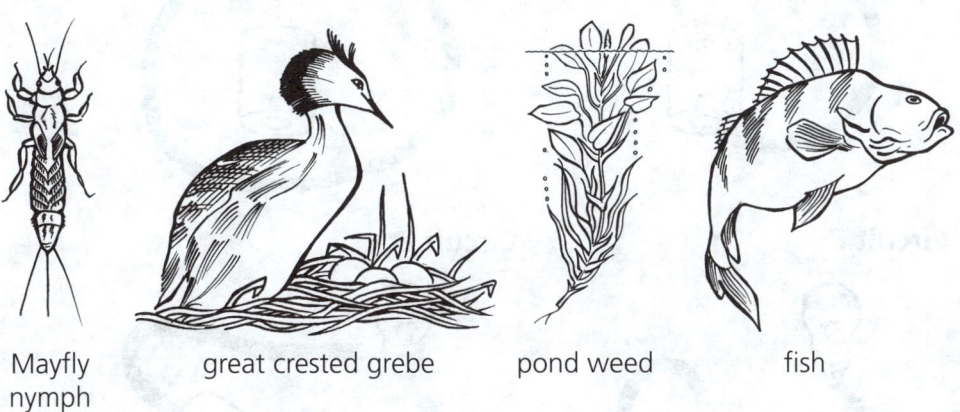

Mayfly nymph   great crested grebe   pond weed   fish

Mayfly nymphs eat pond weed.
Great crested grebes eat fish.
Fish eat mayfly nymphs.

a Write this as a food chain.

.... → .... → .... → ....

Answers can be found on pages 71–73

b Write the name of the producer in the food chain.

....

c Write the name of *two* predators in the food chain.

....

Q13 — 3

Q14 Humans and the three animals in the food chain in Question 13 all move.

Tick *three* boxes that tell you three other things that *all* living animals do.

walk ☐   run ☐

grow ☐   reproduce ☐

swim ☐   feed ☐

Q14 — 3

Q15 Will these circuits light the bulb? Tick the right boxes below.

Circuit A

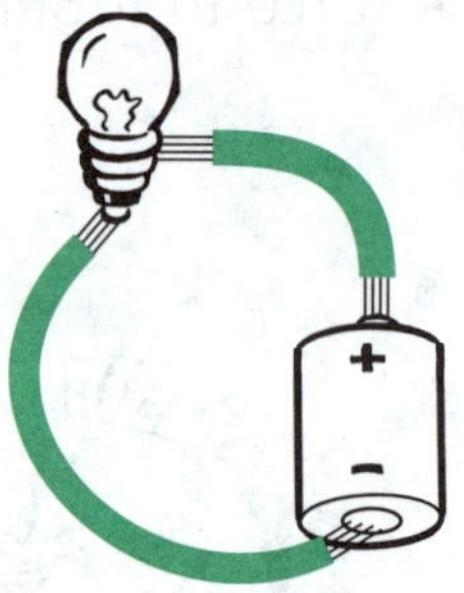

Circuit B

Circuit C

Circuit D

Circuit A	on ☐	off ☐
Circuit B	on ☐	off ☐
Circuit C	on ☐	off ☐
Circuit D	on ☐	off ☐

Q15 — 4

Answers can be found on pages 71–73

Q16 Here are two of the circuits in Question 15 drawn as circuit diagrams. Label the diagrams with letters to match the circuits in Question 15.

Circuit _____   Circuit _____

i   ii

Q17 Steel is a conductor, but if it is coiled into a long spring it can be used as a resistor to alter the current in a circuit.

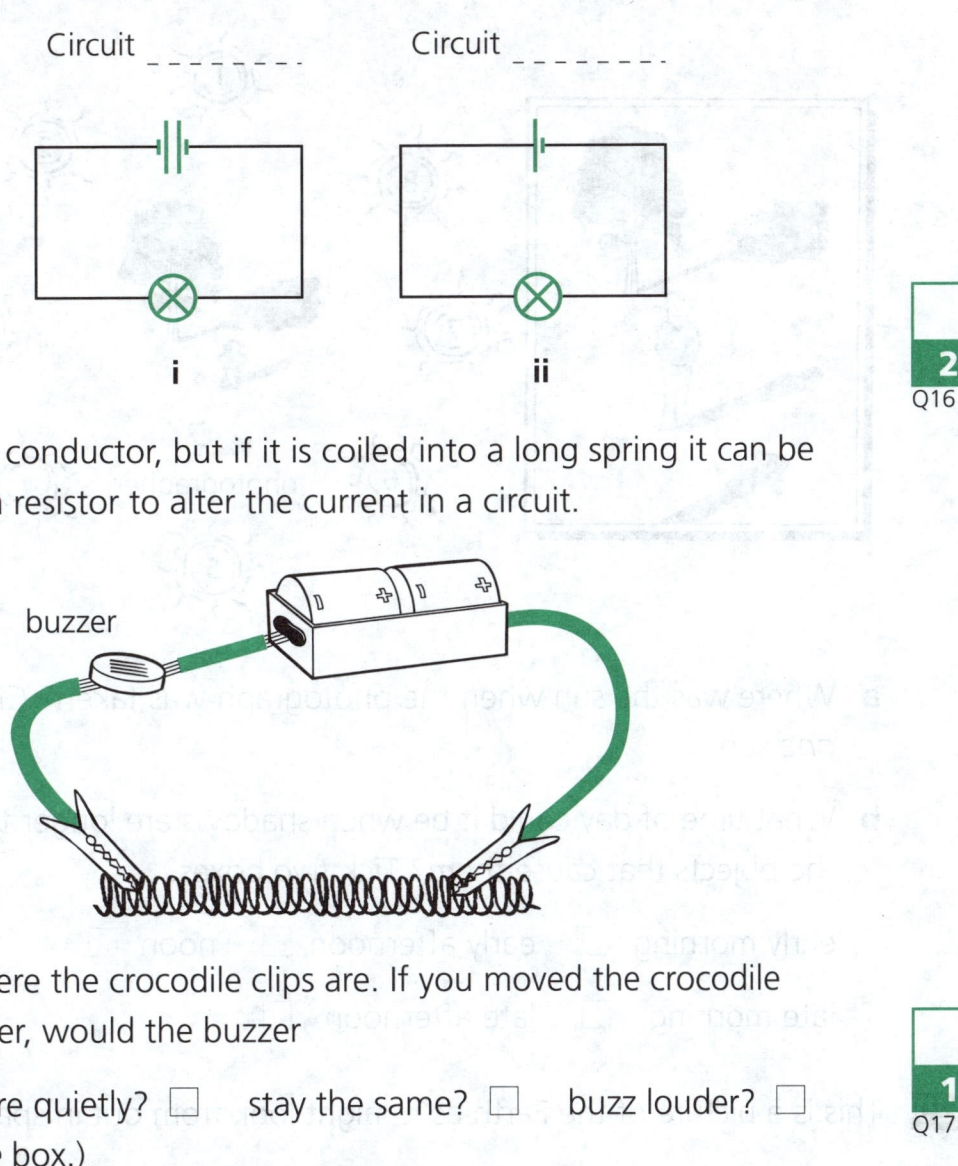

Look where the crocodile clips are. If you moved the crocodile clips closer, would the buzzer

buzz more quietly? ☐   stay the same? ☐   buzz louder? ☐
(Tick *one* box.)

Q18 a Write these spheres in the correct order of size. Begin with the biggest.

  Earth   Moon   Sun

  ....

  b Name the sphere that takes a year to orbit the biggest sphere.

  ....

  c Which sphere completes an orbit approximately every 28 days?

  ....

Answers can be found on pages 71–73

Q19 This is a drawing of a photograph and, beside it, a bird's eye view of the scene as the photograph was being taken.

a Where was the sun when the photograph was taken? Circle *one* sun.

b What time of day could it be when shadows are longer than the objects that cause them? Tick *two* boxes.

early morning ☐   early afternoon ☐   noon ☐

late morning ☐   late afternoon ☐

3
Q19

Q20 This is a picture of the Earth as it might look from out in space.

Sun in position **A**   Sun in position **B**

a In which position would the Sun be? ....

Answers can be found on pages 71–73

At noon in Britain it is midnight in New Zealand. Twelve hours later it will be noon in New Zealand and midnight in Britain.

b Why have night and day changed places?

....

....

Q20

Q21 This is a periscope.

Think about how the light travels when it reflects off a mirror.

What will the boy see? Tick *one* box above.

Q21

Q22 This boy has his ear firmly pressed to the desk, then he taps.

The sound is louder when his ear is touching the desk. Why?

....

Answers can be found on pages 71–73

Q22

Answers: Test A

The level number of each question is given with each answer. The topic number tells you the topic in Part 1 of the book on which the question is based.

Q1 LEVEL 3/TOPIC 1.1
- **a** All plants grow
- **b** All plants reproduce themselves / make copies of themselves

2

Q2 LEVEL 3/TOPIC 3.1
ii v

2

Q3 LEVEL 3/TOPIC 3.1
- **a** no
- **b** The leaves of the plant in the black plastic bag are not getting enough sunlight to make food for the plant

2

Q4 LEVEL 4/TOPIC 2.1
- **a** chocolate bar, chevda (Bombay mix) **b** They both contain a lot of fat

2

Q5 LEVEL 4/TOPIC 1.2
- **A** rampion   **B** gentian   **C** speedwell

3

Q6 LEVEL 5/TOPIC 3.2
- **a** The petals are often brightly coloured to help attract insects to the flower to pollinate it
- **b** The stamen is the male part of the plant; it contains pollen
- **c** The stigma is the female part of the plant; pollen from the stamens must be carried to the the stigma for pollination to take place
- **d** The ovary will grow into a fruit when the stigma has been pollinated

4

Q7 LEVEL 4/TOPIC 2.2
- **a** 3 minutes
- **b** His pulse rate goes up while he is exercising because his heart needs to beat faster. After 3 minutes his pulse rate goes down because his heart does not need to beat so fast when he is not exercising

2

Q8 LEVEL 4/5/TOPIC 6
- **a** The water will evaporate. Some salt will be left in the bottom of the container

2

> **tip** As water evaporates it separates from the solid, leaving the salt as deposits in the bottom of the container.

- **b** Water will evaporate. Water will condense on the underside of the lid and will drip down

2

> **tip** A minature water cycle will form in the closed container B.

Q9 LEVEL 5/TOPIC 9.2
  a gravity, friction
  b The force of gravity will be greater than the force of friction

Q10 LEVEL 3/TOPIC 5
  a shiny paint **b** laminated glass **c** steel **d** rubber **e** rubber

Q11 LEVEL 5/TOPIC 6
  a liquid **b** gas

Q12 LEVEL 3/TOPIC 5
  a marl **b** can't tell **c** The same information provided **d** loam

Q13 LEVEL 4/TOPIC 5
  b liquid **c** solid **d** solid **e** gas **f** gas

Q14 LEVEL 3/TOPIC 5
  a a conductor **b** an insulator

Q15 LEVEL 4/TOPIC 9.1
  a | S | N | S | N | or | N | S | N | S |

  b North and South poles attract each other, but if you try to place similar poles next to each other they repel

Q16 LEVEL 4/TOPIC 7
  a Use a sieve **b** Use filter paper or a fine cloth
  LEVEL 5
  c evaporation **d** vapour **e** heat and stir

Q17 LEVEL 5/TOPIC 7
  a Your ring should follow the patterns of the 9.30 a.m. and 10.30 a.m. rings and should be midway between the two
  b It evaporated
  c Day 2
  d Because water evaporates faster in warm temperatures and the lines are wider apart than on Day 1

Q18 LEVEL 4/TOPIC 7
  a A **b** 20 degrees C

Q19 LEVEL 4/TOPIC 8
  a Circuit 2 **b** Both bulbs would go out
  c stays off **d** glows dimly **e** glows brightly

Q20 LEVEL 4/TOPIC 7
  a Fullest glass gives highest note (H) and emptiest glass gives lowest note (L)
  b Pitch would be higher
  c The tighter the 'string' the higher the note it plays

Answers: Test B

Q1 LEVEL 3/TOPIC 3.1
   a A
   b Plant A has a better root system. The roots on plant B will not be able to get enough water and minerals for the plant. They may not be strong enough to support/hold it properly in the soil

`2`

Q2 LEVEL 3/TOPIC 3.1
   i v

`2`

Q3 LEVEL 3/TOPIC 2.1
   iv v

`2`

Q4 LEVEL 5/TOPIC 2.2
   a arteries **b** veins **c** circulate around the body

`3`

> **tip** *The name given for the flow of blood around the body is the circulatory system. We feel the heart's regular pumping of blood as a pulse at certain points where the blood vessels that carry the blood are close to the skin.*

Q5 LEVEL 4/TOPIC 2.3
They support their bodies and stop them from collapsing
The bones protect the soft, delicate, important internal organs

`2`

> **tip** *Vertebrate is the name given to animals that have a backbone.*

Q6 LEVEL 4/TOPIC 2.3
   a A **b** D

`2`

> **tip** *The muscle at the front of the upper arm that contracts to bend the arm at the elbow is the biceps. The muscle at the back of the arm that expands at the same time is the triceps. When the arm is straightened the triceps contracts and the biceps expands.*

Q7 LEVEL 5/TOPIC 2.2
moisture, warmth

`2`

> **tip** *Seeds do not need sunlight to germinate as they have no leaves at this stage. They do not need to make food while they live off the food store in the seed.*

ANSWERS

Q8 LEVEL 5/TOPIC 2.2
   a They help the air/wind to carry them a distance from the parent plant where they will have a better chance of germinating
   b Animals eat berries and then excrete the seeds later when they are some distance from the parent plant
   c The hard cases protect the seeds for longer, giving more opportunities for them to travel a distance from the parent plant   **3**

Q9 LEVEL 4/TOPIC 6
   a oil, stone   **1**
   b margarine, chocolate, metal   **1**
   c clay, paper, wood, dough   **1**

Q10 LEVEL 4/TOPIC 9.1
   iii   iv   **2**

Q11 LEVEL 4/TOPIC 9.1
   a gravity
   b Water is denser than air so exerts a greater up-force/Water offers more resistance against the down-force of gravity   **2**

Q12 LEVEL 4/TOPIC 9.2
   a upwards   **b** downwards   **2**

Q13 LEVEL 4/TOPIC 4.2
   a pond weed → mayfly nymph → fish → great crested grebe   **1**
   b pond weed   **1**
   c fish, great crested grebe   **1**

Q14 LEVEL 4/TOPIC 1.1
   grow, repoduce, feed   **3**

Q15 LEVEL 3/TOPIC 8
   A on   **B** off   **C** off   **D** off   **4**

Q16 LEVEL 4/TOPIC 8
   i Circuit D   **ii** Circuit A   **2**

Q17 LEVEL 5/TOPIC 7
   buzz louder   **1**

Q18 LEVEL 3/TOPIC 9.3

    a Sun, Earth, Moon   **[3]**

    LEVEL 5

    b Earth **c** Moon   **[2]**

Q19 LEVEL 4/TOPIC 9.3

    a sun 4   **[1]**

    b early morning or late afternoon   **[2]**

Q20 LEVEL 5/TOPIC 9.3

    a A

    b The Earth spins on its axis and after 12 hours the opposite side of the Earth faces the sunlight   **[2]**

Q21 LEVEL 4/TOPIC 10.1

    C

Q22 LEVEL 4/TOPIC 10.3

Sound vibrations travel well through the rigid material of the desk   **[1]**

Marking grid

Test A (pages 47–58)

Question	Marks available	Marks scored
1	2	
2	2	
3	2	
4	2	
5	3	
6	4	
7	2	
8	4	
9	3	
10	5	
11	2	
12	4	
13	5	
14	2	
15	2	
16	5	
17	4	
18	2	
19	5	
20	3	
total	63	

Test B (pages 59–67)

Question	Marks available	Marks scored
1	2	
2	2	
3	2	
4	3	
5	2	
6	2	
7	2	
8	3	
9	3	
10	2	
11	2	
12	2	
13	3	
14	3	
15	4	
16	2	
17	1	
18	5	
19	3	
20	2	
21	1	
22	1	
total	52	

Add your scores from the two tests. The chart on the next page shows how many marks you need to obtain to achieve the National Curriculum levels.

Using the marking grid

	Test A	Test B	Test A+B
Maximum mark	63	52	115
N	0–13	0–10	0–21
Level 2	14–16	11–13	22–28
Level 3	17–32	14–26	29–58
Level 4	33–47	27–39	59–86
Level 5	48+	40+	87+

Level

Mark scored in Test A ☐ → ☐

Mark scored in Test B ☐ → ☐

Total ☐ → ☐